YOUTH WORK AFTER
CHRISTENDOM

YOUTH WORK AFTER CHRISTENDOM

Church, Mission and Working with Young People in a Post-Christendom Age

Jo Pimlott and Nigel Pimlott

Foreword by Stuart Murray
Additional Material by Richard Passmore and Dave Wiles

Paternoster:
thinking faith

MILTON KEYNES ● COLORADO SPRINGS ● HYDERABAD

First published 2008 by Paternoster
Paternoster is an imprint of Authentic Media
9 Holdom Avenue, Bletchley, Milton Keynes, Bucks, MK1 1QR, UK
1820 Jet Stream Drive, Colorado Springs, CO 80921, USA
OM Authentic Media, Medchal Road, Jeedimetla Village, Secunderabad 500
055, A.P., India
www.authenticmedia.co.uk

Authentic Media is a division of IBS-STL U.K., limited by guarantee, with its
Registered Office at Kingstown Broadway, Carlisle, Cumbria CA3 0HA.
Registered in England & Wales No. 1216232. Registered charity 270162

British Library Cataloguing in Publication Data

A catalogue record for this book is available from the
British Library

ISBN-13: 978-1-84227-605-1

Cover design by James Kessell for Scratch the Sky Ltd.
(www.scratchthesky.com)
Print Management by Adare
Printed and bound in Great Britain by J.H. Haynes & Co., Sparkford

Contents

Acknowledgements   vii
Foreword   ix
Background   xi

1. Introduction   1
    What is Post-Christendom?   3

2. Christendom, Youth Work and Young People   8
    The Mindset?   9
    The Context   11
    Sundays!   14
    History   17
    Pesonality and Priesthood   19
    Professional and Postmodern Youth Workers   22
    Youth Work Programmes   24
    Don't Rock the Boat   27
    Schools Work   30
    Colonial Youth Work?   32
    Summer Festivals   36
    Closing Thoughts   38

3. Perspectives on Young People, Life and Spirituality   40
    Respect   41
    Achievements   43
    Behaviour   44
    Health   45
    Expectations   46
    Opportunities   48
    Religion and Spirituality   49
    Other Faith Groups   53

View from the Margins	54
Hope	55
What Are the 'Whys'?	57
Reflections	60
4. Mission: Reching Young People Post-Christendom	62
Integration	63
The Mission of God	65
The Homogenous Unit Principle	68
Incarnational Mission	75
The Message	80
Social Action	86
Community	91
What Will Prevail?	96
5. Resourcing Youth Work Post-Christendom	97
Location, Location, Location	99
Imagine All the People	106
Social Capital	110
Heroes of the Faith	115
Technology	118
New Ideas	123
6. Church Youth Work Post-Christendom	127
Process or Product?	
Growing Church as a Process	133
Working Within the Existing Church	137
Being Open-Edged and Engaging with Contemporary Culture	138
Nurturing Authentic Friendships and Healthy Community	141
Cultivating an Earthed Spirituality Where Young People Encounter God	145
Being Participative, Inclusive and Empowering	149
Holding Deep Convictions but Being Unfazed by Questions and Doubts	151
Stimulating Faith Development at Every Stage of the Journey	153
Closing Thoughts	157
And Finally . . .	159
Endnotes	162

Acknowledgements

We are very grateful to all who have contributed their experience, stories and wisdom to the writing of this book. Our particulr thanks go to students and staff at Midlands Centre for Youth Ministry and all at Frontier Youth Trust.

Foreword

In conversations five years ago within the Anabaptist Network about a series of books on the end of Christendom and the implications of post-Christendom for church and mission in western culture, various subjects were proposed. We anticipated volumes on worship and mission, faith and politics, using the Bible, church life, discipleship and ethics, and several other topics. Some of these have since been published; others are being written and will be published in the next couple of years. But *Youth Work after Christendom* was not on our list.

So when Nigel Pimlott approached me and proposed this additional title, I was both surprised and delighted. Nigel and some of his youth work colleagues had read *Post-Christendom* and had realised that this perspective on mission and culture had many implications for youth work, especially youth work on the margins of society. Youth work, in fact, was another lens through which to investigate the Christendom legacy; just as post-Christendom was a new lens through which to search for appropriate and creative forms of youth work in a changing culture.

As I have watched the book take shape over the past two years, it has been fascinating to learn more about the influence of the Christendom mindset on inherited forms of youth work practice and to imagine with the authors alternative approaches that may be better suited to post-Christendom. Those who engage with young people and youth culture have long been aware of the impact of the cultural shift from modernity to post-modernity. Here is an invitation to take a fresh look at current and future youth work assumptions, expectations and priorities in light of a rather different (though not unrelated) cultural shift.

Nigel and Jo Pimlott bring to this book many years of experience on the cutting edge of youth ministry, relationships with numerous young people and other youth workers (two of whom have contributed to the book) and skills in theological reflection. Their insights, criticisms and proposals are rooted in love for and continuing commitment to a church they find often frustrating but still capable of courage and imagination. Some of their suggestions may seem disturbing – but youth work after Christendom requires a more radical rethink than tinkering with practices that are no longer connecting with young people. Many of their proposals, however, build on the best of current youth work practice and are within reach of churches that are prepared to re-examine what they are doing and why.

If youth culture represents the leading edge of cultural and societal change, or at least reflects the pressures and possibilities emerging in contemporary society, this volume may be one of the most important in the 'After Christendom' series. For if we can re-imagine and re-shape youth work for the emerging post-Christendom culture, perhaps other dimensions of ecclesial and missional transformation will follow.

My hope is that *Youth Work after Christendom* will be an invaluable resource to youth workers, stimulating their thinking and enhancing their ability to engage sensitively and contextually with young people in and beyond the churches. I hope, too, that this volume will introduce post-Christendom perspectives to those who might otherwise not recognise their significance but who will be inspired by reading this book to look at many other dimensions of life and faith from this distinctive angle of vision. And for those who have read the earlier volumes, here is another – maybe unexpected – aspect of mission and discipleship that cannot remain unaffected by the demise of Christendom and the coming of the strange new world of post-Christendom.

Stuart Murray
November 2007

Background

Christian youth work today is in an interesting place. A glance through the job adverts in Christian magazines portrays a vibrant industry offering a wide variety of job opportunities ranging from work in traditional churches and youth clubs to specialist projects, Outward Bound centres, detached settings, mentoring projects and arts-based initiatives. Growing numbers of Christian youth workers are accessing professional training and an army of volunteer workers serves young people and the church on a regular basis, providing a breadth of provision for both Christian young people and those who do not have a Christian faith.

Some churches have a large number of young people, yet many others have seen no young people come through their doors for several years. Christian youth festivals continue to thrive, while regular church attendance appears to be at an all-time low. There are many resources and initiatives to help both youth workers and young people maximize their faith potential and yet the vast majority of young people have little or no contact with a local Christian church.

Young people seem to be experiencing life in unparalleled measure, living fulfilled lives and achieving more at an earlier age than their predecessors. Yet they are demonized by the media and politicians as a bunch of drunken, drug-taking yobs who have life too easy and no respect for adults. They are under pressure to do well academically, contribute to society and save the world! And they are expected to do this while wrestling with changing and confusing family units and dynamics, epidemics of depression and self-harm, a world that is changing more quickly than ever before and a celebrity culture that promises much, but remains largely elusive.

Our experience through many years of undertaking youth work ourselves and through training and supporting churches, organizations and youth workers, is that churches tend to appoint paid youth workers for one of two reasons. Some have a significant number of young people and want an employee to help coordinate the work; others have no young people and hope that by employing a worker their problems will be solved and young people will come back to the church. Both reasons are valid.

But what about the future of Christian youth work? What will it look like in the next few decades? And how has the past way of doing things (both positively and negatively) impacted the way we currently do such work? If it isn't the case already, is working with young people going to be about cross-cultural mission, demanding the same vision, resourcing, preparation and contextualization as mission to a lost tribe or people group? This book considers these questions and many more associated with Christian youth work. It is set against the backdrop of a major change in church and Christian history – that of moving from the era of Christendom to the dawning of the post-Christendom age. We want to argue that this change is exciting, stimulating and full of opportunities while at the same time being potentially daunting, threatening and full of challenge.

1

Introduction

A family friend has a favourite joke. A woman hears on the radio a report of a driver going the wrong way down the M1. Concerned that her husband is on that particular motorway, she calls him on his mobile phone to warn him of the danger. She tells him to be careful as there is someone driving down the carriageway in the wrong direction. He replies, 'There isn't just one person, there's hundreds of them!'

Sometimes youth workers can feel that they are driving the wrong way down a multi-lane motorway with everything else coming at them from the opposite direction. As well as the challenges of working with the young people themselves, with all their energy, hopes, dreams, hurts and frustrations, they find themselves facing the expectations of the church, the anticipation of the minister and the full might of the Parochial Church Council, deacons, leadership team, or whatever other model of church government manifests itself. Added to this, there are often demands from parents who may have transferred their own obligations and placed youth workers in a surrogate role. Then often youth workers also have to cope with the stress that comes from their own desire to fulfil God's mission and calling and build the kingdom in an increasingly secular and hostile world.

Of course, it's not all bad news. Youth work can be one of the most rewarding of all the ministries. Many churches invest significant time, energy and resources into reaching out to and working with young people. The analogy of the motorway, however, reminds us that it's not an easy job and that the context for doing youth work is changing and demanding.

Gone are the days when all young people knew the Christian story. Christian young people now find themselves in a minority among their peer group and often end up on the margins. Young people have left 'Sunday' church in vast numbers over the last few decades. The church has an ageing population and in percentage terms, church attendance in the UK by the 10- to 14-year-old age group is the lowest of any age range.[1] Church attendance in the USA reveals a similarly worrying trend. According to a survey by LifeWay Research, seven out of ten 18- to 30-year-olds who went to church as teenagers had stopped going by the age of 23.[2] Associate Director of LifeWay, Scott McConnell, comments, 'It seems the teen years are like   a free trial on a product. By 18, when it's their choice whether to buy into church life, many don't feel engaged and welcome.'

Evidence of interest in spirituality among young people is at best unclear and at worst not very encouraging.[3] Youthful megachurches pervade some highly populated urban environments, but vast areas of the country have little or no Christian witness and no communities in which young people can share and express their Christian faith in anything like a culturally appropriate environment.

Christianity is now just one faith option when making life choices. The many others range from more traditional religions to a whole range of 'isms' – consumerism, materialism, hedonism, nihilism – that have taken on an almost pseudo-religious status. The following comment is typical of many from youth workers who are wrestling with the changing dynamics of faith, Christianity and young people:

> When I look back at my own days as a young Christian, things were different. We went to the church youth club to learn. We were up for everything to know more about God. Am I just looking back at things with rose-coloured glasses? Did we give the youth workers such a hard time that it made them pull their hair out, like the young people I know now do? Things now do seem to be very different. I run a youth group and I love the kids, but all they seem to want to do is run around the building and break the furniture. It's really hard work.

Of course, when looking back, there is always a danger of the 'grass was greener' syndrome. However, the array of anecdotal evidence that we receive from older youth workers does imply that things have changed. Notwithstanding all this, encouraging stories are emerging of young people finding faith, living out their beliefs, influencing society and developing new forms of church.

This latest book in the *After Christendom* series focuses on the role of Christian youth work in the future.[4] It seeks to explore the influences that the Christendom period has had on the way Christian youth work is currently undertaken, and draws on perspectives based on current work with young people to examine what might happen in the future and offer contextual models for effective mission and ministry with young people. While painting a picture of young people and the culture they live in, we cannot hope, in the space available, to explore in detail the vast cultural changes that have taken place in recent times. Many good books on this subject are already available.

The distinctive nature of this publication is its focus on working with young people in the context of a changing spiritual landscape, and its desire to challenge the impression that 'the Christianity of the land and the Christianity of the New Testament are alike'.[5] Indeed, the probability is that work with young people will exemplify all that is current in culture as they are very often at the forefront of cultural change and, indeed, frequently determine such change. It may also be that those young people who are Christians, and those who work with them, have already embraced the new epoch of post-Christendom as they seek to reconcile their mission and calling with the world around them. We have talked to youth workers and young people about what they think and have included their thoughts throughout the book.[6]

What is Post-Christendom?

The first book in this series provides a full and detailed exploration of post-Christendom.[7] It is beyond the scope of this book to repeat this, but for the purposes of providing a reference point, the following is offered as an historical summary.

The early church was characterized by the refusal of believers to bow to the Roman authorities. This resulted in a martyrs' church. Persecution was widespread and Christianity was essentially a subversive and underground movement. It didn't possess dedicated buildings for worship, and it operated on the margins of society. Its leadership was very much focused around the five-fold ministry gifts declared in Ephesians 4:11. Mission was key and a grassroots' approach underpinned everything that happened.

In 312, when the Roman emperor Constantine converted to Christianity, everything changed. In 313, Constantine and his co-emperor Licinius announced the toleration of Christianity in the Edict of Milan, and the Christian faith moved from being a persecuted faith to being the official religion of the Roman Empire. Buildings became central to worship, leadership hierarchical and institutionalized, and church allegiance essential to ensure success in society and survival under an oppressive regime. From being a faith of the heart, Christianity became a faith of necessity. These changes had consequences that in many parts of the world have influenced the church right up until the present day.

To be specific, the following provides a helpful working definition of post-Christendom:

> Post-Christendom is the culture that emerges as the Christian faith loses coherence within a society that has been definitively shaped by the Christian story and as the institutions that have been developed to express Christian convictions decline in influence.[8]

These changes are illustrated by the following transitions, which are taking place as we move from a Christendom to an increasingly post-Christendom paradigm:

- Movement of the influence of Christianity *from the centre* of life and society *to the margins*.
- From a *majority*, Christians are becoming a *minority* group, force and influence in the western world.
- In Christendom, Christians felt that the world was their home. Our world view had shaped culture and dictated how things were done. We were *settled*. In post-Christendom, Christians

are *sojourners*, who are aliens, exiles and pilgrims in a culture that no longer feels like home.

- In Christendom, Christians enjoyed many *privileges*, but in post-Christendom we are one community among many *pluralistic* others.

- The Christendom stance used to be able to exert *control* over society. Influence only occurs now through *witnessing* (conversing) about our story and its implications.

- Movement from a perspective of *maintaining* what we have and the (supposed) Christian status quo to an emphasis on *mission* in a contested environment.

- Developing churches that in Christendom were in *institutional* mode to those that once again become a Christian *movement*.[9]

Gibbs and Bolger reflect further on these changes:

> [Post-Christendom is] exemplified by pluralism and radical relativism. Religion is understood in terms of its sociological and psychological significance, discounting any claims to divine revelation and absolute truth. Furthermore, the church as an institution has lost its privileged position and increasingly occupies a place on the margins of society alongside other recreational and non-profit organisations.[10]

We will explore the implications of these changes through the lens of youth work and consider the consequences, challenges and opportunities for future work. To help our understanding of what has happened to Christianity and the changes it has undergone from its early roots in the New Testament experience through the establishment of Christendom over the subsequent centuries to the dawning of the post-Christian era, we might use the analogy of soup!

Cooking historians suggest that soup is perhaps one of the oldest forms of food known to humanity. The idea of a liquid food containing various combinations of meat, vegetables, beans, stock and water can be traced back to the Bronze Age. Since then soup has undergone a whole series of developments and processes:

- fresh ingredients prepared over the fire in a cauldron
- ingredients prepared in buildings
- ingredients prepared and canned
- ingredients prepared, condensed and canned
- ingredients dehydrated and put in packets
- ingredients microwaveable
- return to 'fresh' soups.

The versions of soup found in tins are very different from freshly-prepared soups, while those that end up in dehydrated packets bear little resemblance to any other incarnations. A recent examination of the ingredients of a packet chicken soup boldly claimed that it contained 0.5 per cent chicken powder! Throughout these developments, people have continued to make 'real' soup. However, some have preferred the convenience and even the taste of the more processed products. Recently, we have seen an increasing demand for the 'real thing'. Although this may be mass-produced, it is marketed as fresh soup, prepared with real food and containing no e-numbers, artificial colourings or preservatives.

We might draw some parallels here with the development of Christianity. It started off as an authentic honouring of all that Jesus intended, with the early disciples implementing a radical, socially-controversial, subversive, charismatic, serving-and-preferring-one-another faith. Over time, debates about power and political influence, cultural change, use of the faith for people's own ends, association of the faith with respectability, government and education have changed it so considerably that at times it has borne little resemblance to the original.

This analogy inevitably risks gross oversimplification and should not be taken too far. It is clear that throughout the Christendom era many have sought to find and promote 'authentic faith'. There are, however, some interesting parallels. The resurgence of interest in making 'real' soup came at a time when for many the product had ceased to be attractive and people had given up on it. But just as the end was in sight for soup, a few people began to look again at what it was and is all about. They took those original fresh ingredients and began to make great soup again. They gave it a modern and culturally appropriate twist, packaged it in a way people could relate to and sales have taken off. Not only has this approach been successful, but it has spurred others to go back even further in their search for authenticity and to make their own soup. The very radical soup-makers now even grow their own ingredients to ensure that everything that goes into the soup is fresh, free from additives and genuine.

Similarly, people have begun to reject some of the more packaged versions of Christianity that have been on offer in western society and the numbers 'buying' it have fallen to an all-time low. There is a clear need to take action if the current decline is not to continue. Perhaps it is time to go back to the original recipe and take a fresh look at what our 'product' is really all about. This is what many are beginning to do.

2

Christendom, Youth Work and Young People

The story of Eutychus helps focus our thinking.[1] Eutychus was the victim of one of the apostle Paul's long sermons. While Paul was droning on, Eutychus dozed off, fell from the window where he was sitting and plunged down three storeys into the street below, ending up dead. His name means 'fortunate' and he was. Paul responded to the situation with a quick prayerful declaration and Eutychus came back to life.

This story parallels the experience of many young people in today's church. Paul's sermon, however eloquent and anointed, did nothing for Eutychus. We have seen several generations of young people nod off as we have assumed a Christendom mentality and approach when they have increasingly had a post-Christendom mindset.[2] This cannot continue. What worked in the Christendom era and might have been appropriate for that time, no longer works for the vast majority of young people.

So whose fault was it that Eutychus fell? His, for not staying awake and paying attention? Paul's, for going on for so long that he bored Eutychus to death – literally? Or those who did the risk assessment on the suitability of the building for an Alpha course? Casting blame, even if it were possible, serves little useful purpose. What the story does illustrate is that every situation can be seen from a number of different viewpoints. The following illustrations, thoughts and theological reflections are just a number of perspectives on what is a complex subject. The examples are designed not only to highlight the impact of Christendom upon youth work, but to provide material for reflection and further thought. The influence of Christendom is very clear in some respects, while in others it is subtle and harder to define. It is important to emphasize that Christendom cannot be viewed in isolation. It exists alongside other powerful cultural dynamics such as modernism, postmodernism, globalization and constant change. Thus, although we offer the following illustrations, we do not wish to attribute all of the issues to Christendom alone, and we seek to tease out some of the other key influences and backdrops to each.

The Mindset?

> The vicar began the assembly with a rhetorical statement: 'You all know the story of Noah and the ark.' The problem was, the young people didn't.

> A vicar came and did our assembly today. He talked about the Levites. My mate wanted to know why he was talking about jeans (12-year-old).

In this post-Christendom culture, the biblical narrative is no longer the big story by which society and communities operate, but only one of many stories. Youth workers increasingly find themselves working with young people who have little or no understanding of the Christian story. Interestingly, although this is the case in most areas, there are still pockets of communities, normally in working-class, less mobile areas, where children continue to be taught Christian values. In particular, this appears to happen where grandparents have a strong influence. Here they may still bring their grandchildren to church and pass on the stories. This, however, is not the pervading culture in which we operate.

The difficulty is that many people in churches, particularly those who have grown up in a church culture, have still not realized that this huge change has taken place. Within the context of church services, it is to be expected that worship, biblical teaching and approaches to prayer should assume some foundation of Christian knowledge, but in our experience, Christians working in schools and undertaking mission and evangelism in non-church contexts often still expect to be building on an existing knowledge of Christianity. Similarly, many youth workers we talk to struggle to find resources and materials to use with young people outside of and on the edge of church because very many of the resources produced continue to assume some pre-existing biblical knowledge, or are enlightenment-oriented or book-focused.

We see evidence of these assumptions in some of the reactions Christians have had to recent research into young people's spirituality. The research concludes that young people no longer have an interest in spirituality per se and are largely uninterested in spiritual things.[3] However, this is met with incredulity by many Christians, who interpret the wearing of crosses, for example, as interest in spirituality.

The danger of these assumptions, which are caused by a failure to take into account our changing culture, is that for many Christian young people the end result is dualism. Aware of their peers' lack of interest in Christianity, they often find themselves in a difficult place as they try to bridge the cultures of the church and the 'outside' world. They can easily begin to live by one set of standards in a Christian setting and by a different set for the rest of their lives.

When asked about her Christian faith in the setting of school, one young person admitted, 'I didn't have any conversations with school friends as it was all about being cool and such conversations were not cool.' Another commented, 'I didn't broadcast the fact that I was a Christian at school. I felt I couldn't be myself. I did partly live two lives. I did bring friends to events occasionally, but I was leaning towards just being a Sunday Christian.'

Dualism is by no means a new phenomenon. However, we believe it is now exacerbated by the fact that we are in a post-Christendom era. Christians and churches still carrying a Christendom mindset may underestimate, or indeed fail to acknowledge at all, the challenges faced by young people in connecting their faith to the reality of their everyday lives. This sense of disconnection – which is a danger for adults as well as young people – actually accelerates the marginalization of Christianity since it becomes something done as a duty rather than being a living faith, is essentially kept secret, loses everyday contextual dynamic and ultimately becomes a devalued lifestyle choice.

This position is further complicated as young people end up bridging the modern and postmodern eras, yesterday's and tomorrow's worlds, and potentially carry the angst and frustrations of the failings (with relation to mission and kingdom-building) of the adults who work with them.

A recent experience – one of a number we have had during youth work training sessions – highlighted the different worlds of Christendom and post-Christendom in a very stark way. On this occasion, some youth workers who had grown up with a Christendom mindset got very angry and defensive when post-Christendom was talked about. They felt that to speak of such things was to be anti-church, to betray the faith and to criticize all that had gone before. For one group this all proved too much and they decided to boycott future sessions! However, on the same course, children of the post-Christendom era reflected that the training session talked about the real world, told it how it was, liberated them, spurred them to mission, contextualized the good news and provided momentum to grow church.

The Context

> When the youth service had finished and the coffee was being served, the silver-haired woman remarked to the youth worker, 'It's so lovely to see so many young people in church today.'

The world of young people is increasingly global, pluralist and diverse. It is a world where change is constant and faith choices and practices are as transitory as everything else. Religious allegiance is the same – the Christian of today might be a Buddhist tomorrow and an atheist the day after. The world of celebrity, which often sets the pace, confirms these fluctuations, with high-profile stars declaring allegiance to particular beliefs one minute and abandoning them the next. The impact of these beliefs upon lifestyle is at best short-lived and often hard to determine.

This world stands in stark contrast to that of the Christendom era, where societal structures and belief systems have remained static for many years. Styles of church worship might ebb and flow, but even in the most modern of churches basic patterns of church worship have remained largely unaltered for several hundred years. Clearly this reluctance to embrace change cannot be laid solely at Christendom's door. Resistance to change is by no means a recent phenomenon and throughout history we see evidence of the common human trait to wish to preserve things as they are.

What is important to acknowledge here, though, is the way in which the Christendom mindset established habits of thinking and being that in many churches are now regarded as beyond question. Many of the practices, values and attitudes pervasive today – particularly those related to leadership and worship – were embedded in the church during the Christendom era. There is consequently a very real sense in which leaders and people in many churches and denominations have a heavy investment in the Christendom mindset since this is the source of their power, authority and raison d'être. When this is combined with the natural human inclination to preserve the status quo, it is evident that change might not be the highest item on everyone's agenda.

If the 'world our kids are going to live in is changing four times faster than our schools',[4] we suspect it is changing many more times faster than our churches. The expectation that young people should fit into these established church patterns seems fundamentally flawed, given their wider experience and culture.

Interestingly, in an ever-changing, transitory culture, more rooted expressions of faith and worship might be embraced and valued as anchors to provide stability and security in the midst of constant flux. This is reflected in the resurgence of interest in ancient forms of worship – such as Celtic and Orthodox – and in the growing interest within emerging forms of church in more ritualistic approaches to spirituality. However, we believe this needs to work hand in hand with an understanding of and response to the culture in which young people live. Contextualization is key.

All too often, the gap between what is communicated in church and young people's experiences of the everyday challenges of life is just too wide to be bridged. Christian young people are already in the minority and often experience bullying or teasing because of their faith. This potentially gives them a vivid perspective on what post-Christendom is all about. However, often they are not being effectively equipped to live in such a world. In the following extract, Brendon's anger swells at the failure of his youth group to give him the answers he needs. The Christianity it offers is not spiritually satisfying. It is not ethically satisfying. It is not even fun.

> They try to pump you full of morals but they don't have any clue what you are going through – like all the problems I feel with hate for school, and the problems I experience with my family and cynicism for God. They just naturally expect you to be Christian because your parents are and you go to church.[5]

Triumphalistic theologies and approaches risk making life worse for young people since they contrast sharply with the bullying, mickey-taking and abuse that often goes hand in hand with being a Christian in school. This environment can be very hostile towards young kingdom-seekers. Rarely does their experience reflect the ideology of a powerful, influential, growing church, an ideology that is often still preached, particularly by churches with an evangelical and/or charismatic flavour where church members may be in denial about the end of Christendom. If the message received by young people is that 'faith' is all that is needed to overcome difficulties, then they can feel a sense of failure when their difficulties are not overcome. What was a bad situation ends up becoming worse.

Sessions on 'how to handle persecution' don't often appear in youth work curricula, yet persecution is frequently what young people experience. One youth worker recently told how a young person had given up his faith because of the hostility he had experienced at school. We look with admiration and humility at Christians on other continents who have withstood persecution, yet the western Christendom mindset has influenced youth work to the extent that we have not even acknowledged, never mind admired, young people in this country who have stood tall for their faith. We haven't even begun to develop support, theologies and strategies for those young people for whom the battleground has become too hostile and who have decided that living as marginalized believers is just too difficult to maintain.

Sundays!

Given a blank sheet of paper, most young people would probably say that early on a Sunday is one of their least favourite times for a church service, yet this model of meetings persists throughout most of the western world. In the UK, many young people have voted with their feet and stopped going. Even in the USA, where church attendance is still relatively high among the general population, young people are going less and less often. Research indicates that in 1997, 53 per cent of teens went to a worship service. By 2007, this figure had fallen to 48 per cent.[6]

In the early church, many Jewish Christians continued to attend the synagogue on Saturdays. But Sunday, although a working day, became a focal point for the emerging church to gather to eat and pray. Subsequently, Constantine institutionalized Sunday as *the* time for corporate gathering for prayer and worship, a state of affairs that became the norm through the Christendom era. This sabbathization of Sundays, undertaken for political purposes, is the legacy that remains today. For many churches, success, attendance, belonging and commitment are all measured in relation to the Sunday meeting or service. So much energy goes into the Sunday expression of church that the two hours on a Sunday often appear to be the be-all and end-all for many Christian communities.

Issues, debates and conflicts around what happens in Sunday gatherings have disillusioned many a committed and enthusiastic youth worker. The current approach to Sundays robs other expressions of being church of resources and both spiritual and natural energy. Very often it is the youth budget that suffers most!

> One of church growth's primary tools is to coax people into a special place once a week where God is the focus of the entire event. The idea is that if people will think of God for a few hours on Sunday, maybe they'll also consider him the other 166 hours

during the week. All manner of resources are expended to make these few hours as efficient and relevant as possible . . . The amount of blood, sweat, prayer and tears extended in this paradigm is extraordinary.[7]

Although our experience would suggest that most young people do not engage with Sunday services, many youth workers still find that the expectation of the church is that a significant aspect of their role is to get the young people into church at all costs. The 'bums on seats' approach remains the measure of success in many church contexts. One consequence is that attendance at meetings is overemphasized at the expense of focusing on mission, developing shalom and building the kingdom. Len Hjalmarson writes:

In our modern Christian culture we are building centred and leader centred. The result is that we have become very passive and dependent. We even began to believe that Sunday was the centre of our lives, and we began to see Sunday as a Holy day and the church building as a Holy place. We were near to idolatry. With a new Temple at the centre of our belief system, we built many 'Come' structures. We even rebuilt Old Testament worship, and talked about the 'sanctuary' as though God lived in buildings made with hands. With the huge effort and expense of maintaining a physical structure, all roads led to 'Rome'. We had many ways to call people together in the fortress, and many programs to keep them busy. This took care of most of our free time, so we had to hope that unbelievers would come to us.

But they didn't come. The more needy ones didn't even feel welcome. With all our formalism (it's there, even if you don't see it), how could they? Not only did they lack the right clothes or the right language, they certainly didn't have the right habits or etiquette.

With all our 'Come' structures, we had no 'Go' structures. We had many roads leading to the fortress, but no roads that led outward into our communities. We weren't involved in the lives of our neighbours; we were far too busy with church things. Our lives revolved around buildings and programs and other Christians. While we felt very comfortable, we were isolated from the real world Jesus entered and had no way to connect with the lost ones around us.[8]

When seeking to employ a youth worker or to develop their work with young people, many churches still look for someone who will maintain the status quo, and underpin the existing 'come' structures of the church. Youth workers with a heart for mission and a desire to meet young people where they are at often become disillusioned when they confront these expectations. We have supported many youth workers who are pushing boundaries regarding fundamental questions about church, youth ministry and the role and function of youth work in developing church and mission. Sadly, our role has often been to patch up those who have been reined in from activities that have not involved babysitting the children of existing church members, and who have been criticized when they have been brazen enough to involve churched young people in activities that encourage direct contact with young people outside the church, who may be a 'bad' influence.

The Sunday factor impinges upon the rest of the youth worker's week. Because Sunday is seen as the day for worship, attempts to facilitate worship at other times are often demeaned. More radical attempts to reframe worship into active service of others (Rom. 12:1) or into faith-based activity, are all too often frowned upon or nipped in the bud as 'unsound' or as placing too much emphasis on a 'social gospel'.

'Serious' teaching, 'proper' worship, major relationship development and fostering of community are often perceived to be Sunday activities. While many would deny this, failed attempts to change the paradigm will probably confirm that it is the case. The result is that young people end up being pushed to the margins and largely ignored.

In a fast-moving culture where recreational activity rather than restorative rest is often the order of the day, there is evident need for a 'Sabbath-rest for the people of God'.[9] Christendom's legacy would appear to be a Sunday 'Sabbath' tied to societal expectations, good citizenship and respectability. For young people today the need is surely for expressions of Sabbath rest that work for them and forms of meeting that take their culture into account. In terms of gathering together, Acts 20:7 speaks of the believers meeting on the first day of the week to break bread. Elsewhere, the book of Acts gives vibrant snapshots of the early church gathering together daily for prayer, worship and breaking bread.[10] The challenge as we see it is to provide approaches to gathering that are meaningful to young people, and that provide whole-life, connected opportunities for worship, prayer, ministry and support.

It is helpful to consider what young people's current experiences of Sunday services might be. Some questions to reflect upon might include:

- What is the purpose of Sunday worship? Who is it aimed at?
- To what extent do young people participate – are they allowed to pray for adults?
- In what ways are young people regularly involved in preaching or leading worship?
- In what ways do adults value young people's attendance, good behaviour and conformity above belief, process, values and sense of being on a faith journey?
- Are youth services genuine attempts to hear and learn from young people or are they tokenistic offerings to appease and pacify?
- What happens when young people wish to do communion differently? Are they allowed to bring in a sense of joy, celebration, noise and creativity?

History

Modern-day top football clubs would seem to have little to do with Christendom. Awash with money, owned by international billionaire entrepreneurs and with players as likely to appear on the front pages of the newspapers as the back, the sport has unparalleled global popularity among young and old alike. The roots of the game, however, have, in some cases, grown out of the principles of youth work and the influence of Christendom. Manchester City Football Club, for instance, was founded in 1880 by a rector's daughter, Anna Connell, and two churchwardens from St Marks Church in West Groton, Manchester. Their motivation was to establish something that would stop young people getting into trouble and help keep them out of the pubs! Peter Lupson recounts that at least ten other clubs were founded by churches.[11]

Christians pioneered what we now call youth work. Motivated by compassion for those children and young people who were poor, uneducated, ignored by society and at risk of being exploited, and concerned about the drunkenness, violence and poverty of the working classes and the impact this was having upon the young people from those families, philanthropic, church-going men and women established youth clubs to combat such ills and to provide opportunities for development and learning. The emergence in the eighteenth and nineteenth centuries of the Sunday school movement and the beginnings of organizations such as the YMCA are defining reference points in the history of youth work.

Discipline, education, drill classes, moral and religious instruction were the usual elements of the curriculum on offer as these middle-class reformers sought to alleviate poverty and highlight the benefits to industrialists and power-brokers of having a more educated, controlled and manageable working class. The theory was that a young person in education, instruction and under discipline was more likely to make a better employee than someone who was drunk, wayward and violent.[12]

The impact of Christendom upon these developments cannot be overstated. Early expressions of youth work were often regimented and they gave birth to uniformed movements that took on a militaristic feel, something that still remains today, as can be seen at events such as Remembrance Day parades, where uniformed groups of young people stand alongside the armed forces, clergy and secular leaders and figureheads. We see clearly in these early youth work movements a sense of compassion for the lost, destitute and abandoned, and a desire to help young people find their place as members of society. They also carried strong elements of putting young people on the 'straight and narrow', 'cleaning them up', and 'teaching them respect'.

All societies seek to socialize the young. Indeed, socialization is an essential part of child and adolescent development. What happened within the Christendom era, however, was that

Christendom values were built into the fabric and culture of the emerging youth organizations, and socialization in a youth work context was institutionalized. For the young people concerned, involvement in youth work became synonymous with good citizenship, church attendance and adherence to 'Christian' values and behaviour.

People who attended Sunday school in the late nineteenth to mid-twentieth centuries tell numerous tales of fearsome Sunday school teachers who were not to be messed with. Control and discipline were the order of the day. A relative recalls an experience from the 1940s where he and his siblings were marched to church by their father, who walked behind them with a big stick and hit them on the legs if they talked or misbehaved. Perhaps unsurprisingly, these attendees and their children were those who later began to leave church in unprecedented numbers.

The legacy of this focus on social and moral instruction is evident in both our education system and our approaches to youth work and has both positive and negative elements. From a positive point of view, we can see the value in encouraging young people to embrace Christian values and take their place in society. In Christian youth work contexts, however, controlling young people's behaviour can still be emphasized at the expense of promoting creative, innovative and expressive work that helps them focus upon their spiritual journey and holistic development.

It is interesting to consider these issues in the current political climate where there is unparalleled emphasis on getting young people off the streets, controlling anti-social behaviour and teaching respect. Many churches have supported these government policies, and, with the encouragement of the government, have been at the forefront of delivering such youth work.[13] This use of faith-based organizations to deliver government policy is somewhat resonant of the close allegiance between church and state seen throughout the Christendom era.

Personality and Priesthood

The priesthood of all believers (1 Pet. 2:9) seems to have been a given in the early church. All the believers were charged with the responsibility of growing the kingdom, and while some disciples clearly had leadership responsibilities, the fledgling church was seen as one body with every 'priest' carrying out an essential function (Rom. 12:4–8; 1 Cor. 12:12–30).

The way in which leadership structures were established and grew in complexity during the Christendom era has been described elsewhere, but it is important to note that its legacy remains today in certain aspects of church leadership and government. A hierarchical approach to leadership and church governance is one aspect of this legacy, as is the distinction between clergy and laity, which can also be seen – although the terms used are different – in newer streams and denominations. This emphasis on the 'professional' clergy has given us a hierarchy of priesthood that has ultimately become enshrined in both national and church law. We have archbishops, bishops, canons, ministers, vicars and pastors, to name but a few, and additional paid roles such as counsellors, youth ministers and children's workers. Moves to ordain youth workers seem likely to increase the distinctions still further.

In some church cultures, the separation of laity and clergy (in the broadest understanding of the terms) has led to leadership being perceived almost as a 'holy grail'. This has combined with the emergence of a type of youth ministry focused around personal charisma, perhaps connected to the celebrity culture, to produce a Christian culture in which some youth workers have an almost ethereal status, often based more upon the strength of their personality than on service and compassion. There is nothing wrong with personality, and the kingdom needs such people. The danger lies in the possibility of youth workers becoming Pied Piper figures leading young people to the promised land. As one youth worker commented, 'Too many youth work events and projects are dependent upon the personality of the youth worker and rely upon nepotism in order to sustain them.'

In the Christendom model, clerics often had social influence and power. Vestiges of this model can still be seen in certain approaches to leadership and church discipline. To young people who have grown up in the postmodern culture, which expresses little trust in or respect for authority structures, these ways of working can feel particularly anachronistic and peculiar. Some of these strands of thinking combine with contemporary secular cultural influences to ensure that the types of youth work that are most valued is often those with the best marketing campaigns, the biggest budgets, the highest profiles and the most effective PR and media contacts. Sadly, nepotism in the church did not die out after the intervention of Martin Luther and others, but rather continues to pervade many youth work organizations and churches.

> Christendom . . . has a very fixed notion of the church . . . It is normally associated with buildings and clergy. Its missional mode is primarily attractional rather than sending or incarnational . . . Its type of leadership can generally be described as priestly, sometimes prophetic to insiders but almost never to outsiders (no one 'out there' is listening) and rarely apostolic.[14]

Clearly some are called to leadership within the church, but while acknowledging that, it is interesting to consider how leadership should work in the postmodern, post-Christendom context. There is a need to bridge the clergy–laity divide and to seek to encourage a greater understanding of the priesthood of all believers. Interestingly, as more Christian youth workers are professionally trained, with a consequent greater awareness of community work principles of empowerment and participation, dilemmas are raised for those working within hierarchical leadership structures. We would argue that such principles and values are to be found in the life and work of Jesus. However, many youth workers wishing to adopt a more facilitative approach to their ministry find themselves under pressure, perhaps from other leaders within the church, or simply through the culture of their organizations, to adopt a more hierarchical approach.

Dwindling resources and numbers may well force youth workers to develop their thinking around this issue still further. Many have talked about discipling those who are not yet Christians, as Jesus appears to have done. The missional demands of the coming era may well need non-believers as much as believers to build the kingdom. This is theologically and practically challenging, but has some biblical precedence. For example, in Luke 19, were the owners of the colt required by Jesus believers? And in Acts 8 and 9, was God using Saul to scatter the believers – which was the making of the early church? Saul was an unbeliever, but later God clearly had his hand on him.

Professional and Postmodern Youth Workers

REBEL ROUSER WANTED

To stir up bored young people to cause social revolution and transformation

Only those filled with the Holy Spirit and able to handle intense persecution need apply

---

A glance at youth work job adverts in Christian magazines is very revealing. Most want 'lively', 'energetic', 'inspiring' and 'enthusiastic' people. These qualities are commendable, but betray further evidence of a desire not to rock the boat. The fact remains that most churches and Christian organizations want a 'safe' appointment. Adverts, such as the fictitious job advert above, that seek 'shaker of the suburbs', 'upsetter of the religious and pious', and 'anti-war-and-injustice worker' are few and far between. Equally, we rarely see adverts asking for 'quiet', 'compassionate' and 'sensitive' youth workers. While they clearly have a role to play, they appear not to be in demand in our rather one-dimensional approach to youth work.

Over recent years, increased opportunities for churches to access funding have led to more work being undertaken with marginalized young people and in social action contexts. The vast majority of job adverts, however, are still for churches in wealthy middle-class areas. The needs of the suburbs dominate. These churches tend to have the most money and pay higher salaries. Their success is to be celebrated, but this success does nothing for those who are on the edge. Those who have get more, and those who have little risk the erosion of the little they have. This pattern will continue unless there is significant investment into inner cities, isolated rural areas, and the numerous pockets of deprivation that are to be found throughout the UK. If the post-Christendom church is to take this issue seriously, then partnership work needs to increase so that richer churches invest into more needy areas. If this doesn't happen, marginalization will accelerate and any possibility of bridging the gap between the youth work of the Christendom and post-Christendom eras will be severely restricted.

A further factor that might be viewed as a threat to mission in a post-Christendom era is the professionalization of youth work. This is a relatively recent phenomenon and cannot therefore be wholly laid at Christendom's door. However, aspects of the Christendom legacy – the institutionalization of leadership structures and the divide between clergy and laity – can be seen in this trend. Professionalism in youth work has many benefits, including a workforce with better skills, individuals with a clearly defined vocation, improved management of work, people with more time and the ability to work with other professionals on an equal footing. Care needs to be taken, however, both to avoid a valuing of 'professional' ministry at the expense of encouraging the involvement of the wider body of Christ, and to ensure that professionalism does not become a place of power, protected by jargon, institution and structure.

There is a clear difference between adopting good professional practice, which seeks excellence, safe spaces for young people to be, reflection, learning and growth, and allowing the kind of professionalization that:

- creates dependence on paid staff and disempowers volunteers who then no longer volunteer;
- causes a congregation to abdicate its responsibility to young people, expecting the paid professional to do all that is required;
- engenders unrealistic expectations with regard to growth, good practice and attendance at Sunday services;
- is costly and unattainable for some with a vision and heart for youth work;
- reinforces the sense of church as an institution as opposed to a movement;

- takes a short-term approach: many professionals have contracts of only two to three years, which can be very destructive for the worker, young people and the communities they live in.

Kierkegaard describes priests as 'cannibals' and says they must be stopped.[15] He castigates anyone who 'profits by, lives off and gets promoted by' working for Christianity. While his comments are perhaps extreme, his attack on this aspect of Christendom is interesting to consider in a context in which many churches and Christian agencies are struggling financially. Many excellent youth work projects have simply stopped when the funding has ceased, leaving the young people high and dry. This aspect of professionalization is rarely addressed and is in urgent need of remedying. Many denominations are currently facing resource shortages and sadly the budgets allocated to youth work are often among the first to be cut. What will happen when the money does run out – as it will, if numerical attendance and giving continue to decline – and we once again have to rely solely on volunteers to work with young people?

Youth Work Programmes

Jesus didn't have a course or a programme to put people on. He also appeared unconcerned about how many people showed up for anything he did. He focused on journeying together and working informally. He concentrated on growth, learning and development rather than structure, qualifications and head knowledge. Living the learning was the most important thing.

The Christendom era saw church-based learning focused on church and 'churchy' things at the expense of mission and journey. Our youth work programmes are often clouded by middle-class values that promote settling, achievement and behavioural stability rather than adventure, movement and discovery. Delivery of programmes focuses on gathering young people in an attraction-centred, conversion-focused way rather than developing methodologies that embrace on-the-job and on-going discipleship models.

Many youth workers, particularly volunteers with little time, find 'ready-to-use' material for meetings helpful. This can be useful, but needs to be contextualized. For some groups Alpha courses work well, for others they don't. Workers expecting to import such programmes without first translating them into the local culture and context will find them of little value. It is interesting to note how many youth ministry resources and models are imported from the United States, a culture which, broadly speaking, is not as far into the post-Christendom transitions as the UK. This again highlights the need for home-grown resources that engage with young people in their culture and do not assume an existing knowledge of Christianity.

Sadly, many programmes are imposed from the top down and take little account of young people's views, interests and needs. The end result is often frustrated youth workers and fed up young people. Even when successful, such programmes are prone to producing young people who are clones. While these young Christians can often operate within specific contexts – a particular organization or denomination – they are ill-equipped for mission or the wider world. Consequently, too many young people lose their faith when they undergo a social or life change such as going to secondary school, university or starting a job.

Jesus is often portrayed as the model for life and work. However, it is the Christendom paradigm that has influenced the model that has come down to us. This has emphasized certain aspects of Jesus' life and character at the expense of others. Questions around whether young people should 'belong, believe or behave' first have influenced many youth work programmes negatively, the overemphasis on ethics, morals and behaviour putting too many young people off Christianity for good. These young people have interpreted Christianity as a faith that doesn't like certain people (typically, homosexuals, people who have sex outside marriage, and anyone who drinks alcohol and likes fun), and they have little understanding about what the faith is really all about.

The influence of the Christendom era in erroneously promoting the desire to control and encourage conformity has led youth workers and church leaders to concentrate upon messages about their understanding of 'holy living' at the expense of 'living life to the full' (Jn. 10:10). The result is again that some young people are put off Christianity while those who embrace it end up feeling guilt-ridden. One young person eloquently summarized some of the tensions:

> Modern church has some funny ideas. I could go to church and I can gossip about someone, but I can't light up a cigarette. That's hypocritical. People see Christianity by what the church does . . . The church way is not the Christian way. A lot of the time it's skewed . . . People are angry at what the church has done, not what the Bible says . . . the result is that God gets blamed for what the church does.

Another young person said, 'The image of the church is a problem because people don't have a message from the church that they can understand.'

The difficulties are exemplified by the experience of a church in the Midlands. This church had a very real sense of calling and the energy and momentum to work with the young people who lived nearby. The vicar and his curate were young and enterprising and successfully engaged a number of young people from very diverse ethnic backgrounds. The church congregation began to rise to the demands of working with these young people, who often presented challenging behaviour. They befriended them and from working with them on the streets began to invite them to activities and sessions in the church hall.

The young people responded positively and started to come into the building on a regular basis. They often ran around the room and frequently tried to get into the adjoining church worship area. The congregation exerted a great deal of energy in policing the building to stop this exuberant behaviour. Soon the invitation was given to the young people to come along to a Sunday worship service. Then things got interesting!

The young people, who couldn't relate at all to what went on in the service, talked, laughed, made a lot of noise and ran around the building. The congregation were not happy. The complaints began to arrive on the vicar's and churchwardens' doormats, emails and telephone answering machines. Attempts were made to remedy the situation, but not to the satisfaction of the congregation.

The young people saw the building as part of their community, they had become involved in the life of the church and some were even coming to the Sunday services, but it was not turning out as the enthusiastic missionaries had imagined. They had anticipated that the young people would behave like them. They didn't.

To cut the story short, the tensions could not be overcome. A decision was made to stop working with the young people and to end the relationships. In summary, the people had prayed about young people in their community and God had answered and enabled effective mission to take place. However, because the congregation did not contextualize what they were doing, or embrace a willingness to change to receive the young people, the gap between them proved too big to bridge. One can only imagine what the young people now think of church and Christianity. The lessons were very painful for all involved.

In later chapters, we will examine how youth work programmes might be more geared to following a 'Jesus as model', rather than an institutionalized educational approach and we will explore how mission might look when tragedies such as this are avoided.

Don't Rock the Boat

> Churches aren't very good generally at releasing people and empowering them. They are really bad at releasing young people (Youth worker).

It is fairly broadly acknowledged that in the Christendom era Jesus and his teaching were somewhat marginalized in favour of a morality drawn from the Old Testament and the epistles.[16] This was particularly true in the case of issues around relationships with authority – whether secular or ecclesiastical. Thus, in the teaching of the church, conformity rather than revolution tended to be the order of the day. There was little enthusiasm for a Jesus who confronted the authorities, challenged injustice, spoke up for the marginalized and criticized the religious elite.

In one sense, it is evident that many cultures would be reluctant to encourage their young people to rock the boat. The Christendom era, however, enabled conformist values to become so embedded within the culture of the church that they continue to be pervasive, at least implicitly, if not explicitly, in many churches, particularly with regard to attitudes towards young people. Models of working and ways of being have tended to promote compliance rather than radical thinking, obedience rather than questioning and are linked by many people to morality and personal holiness.

Theoretically, Christian leaders often see empowerment as a positive concept, but really to empower means to relinquish control. Church leadership and power have tended to go hand in hand, and giving up any of this power can feel threatening to those who use it as a base for their security, position and profile. As the above comment from a youth worker suggests, the idea of releasing people is challenging for many churches. It is important to recognize the tension between releasing young people and maintaining a power base. Letting young people loose is often scary for churches and church leaders.

Many Christian young people wear WWJD (What Would Jesus Do?) wrist-bands. I have never heard of any being encouraged by youth workers, or anyone else for that matter, to go on a rampage in their local cathedral, church hall or Christian conference centre to protest against unfair or ungodly financial policies. They are rarely urged to challenge school authorities on issues of justice, are never encouraged to demonstrate in church about the lack of young people's involvement in Sunday services, and the idea of missing school to protest about a war was recently frowned upon by many people.

Speaking about Paul's encounters at Ephesus, which caused a riot among the local people (Acts 19:23,29), and frustrated by our relative apathy, Rob Bell, the leader of Mars Hill Bible Church in Michigan, propagated the idea that what we need is a radical, revolutionary approach: 'Have you signed up for the revolution, but are now running a spiritual business?'[17] His appeal is for youth leaders to rediscover the revolutionary traits that transformed the idol-worshipping citizens of Ephesus into followers of Jesus.

Hirsch highlights the importance of constantly critiquing the structures and rituals we develop and maintain, but suggests that rather than a very negative, anti-establishment approach, we should adopt what he calls a form of 'holy rebellion'

> based on the loving critique of religious institution modelled by the original apostles and prophets – 'holy rebels' who constantly attempted to throw off encumbering ideologies, structures, codes and traditions that limited the freedom of God's people and restricted the gospel message that they are mandated to pass on . . . It is rebellion because it refuses to submit to the status quo. But because it is holy rebellion, it directs us towards a greater experience of God than we currently have.[18]

Mission can cause trouble. It should lead to transformation and social change. Yet today, mission with young people rarely invites social change, tending instead to concentrate on theologies of conversion rather than journeys of discipleship and discovery. It presumes that young people are 'spiritually ripe', just waiting for someone to tell them about Jesus. Then they will make a commitment of faith and everything will be okay. Nothing could be further from the truth.

Often, when youth workers undertake mission in a school, community or youth club, they present a brief synopsis of the gospel. If the young people respond, they are told about a local church, an activity or series of events that they can attend. If they don't respond, they are often abandoned as though they never existed. In doing this, the youth workers are selling the young people short of the fullness of the message of Jesus. They:

- avoid the basic duty of journeying with young people;[19]
- fail to deal with the many questions that young people might have, which might cause youth workers and churches problems (for example, issues about sexuality, debt, suffering, the environment, drug taking);
- stop short of having a two-pronged approach of both telling about the basics of the gospel, and challenging the inequalities, injustices and plight of many people (including young people)

in churches, the community and society as a whole; and thus
- reinforce a dualistic approach to faith.

The dominant hermeneutic (way of interpreting the biblical texts) has led to things being done in an ordered and structured way rather than in a dynamic, rebellious, radical way. Control has proved to be more desirable than change. In charismatic circles, the Holy Spirit has been restricted to a personal development role, with prophetic engagement with society and its problems and issues sadly lacking. So young people have been encouraged to declare prophetic words of encouragement rather than words of loving condemnation about injustice and poverty. Mass marches to Make Poverty History are acceptable, but heckling, demonstrations of God's displeasure (such as those of Jeremiah, Amos and Obadiah) and graffiti protest (perhaps like that in the book of Daniel) are treated with disdain and disapproval, and painted with a broad 'anti-social behaviour' brushstroke. No doubt most biblical prophets, preachers and mission-makers would have been served with anti-social behaviour orders if they had been around today. Dave Andrews writes:

> The essential problem in any situation of injustice is that one human being is exercising control over another and exploiting the relationship of dominance. The solution to the problem is not simply to reverse the roles . . . [but] for people to stop trying to control each other.[20]

If we stopped trying to control young people then maybe they would rock the boat for the sake of the kingdom. We could do with it.

Schools Work

It is perhaps schools work that most clearly exemplifies the link between Christendom and youth work. In the last few decades, the number of Christians visiting schools has risen dramatically. Christians take lessons and assemblies, run lunchtime clubs and may be involved in mentoring schemes, learning support initiatives, sports, music and drama programmes and many other expressions of work with pupils.

There are currently debates about whether such schools work is about education or evangelism, whether it is appropriate to do mission to what, in essence, is a captive audience and whether such work is a gross abuse of power by youth workers. Thankfully, most people who visit schools to undertake this work appear to be motivated by the desire to serve the school and help the young people. If, however, they feel that doing such work is a legal right, they have succumbed to the influences of Christendom in a particularly alarming way.

In England, churches, Christian organizations, youth and schools workers often appeal to the law of the land when seeking to work in schools. It is clearly laid out in statute that each school should have a 'daily act of collective worship which should be of a broadly Christian nature'.[21] In reality, most schools can't logistically do this and the statute is largely ignored. This legal right causes much angst in schools and for those who have to implement this law in what is usually a secular or multi-faith context.[22] Some Christians see schools as a battleground and are incredulous when they are prevented from communicating the gospel there. Such privileges are tied to a Christendom mindset and history.

Writing back in 1990, Janet King commented:

> The inclusion of the phrase 'wholly or mainly of a broadly Christian character' in reference to school worship indicates a genuine desire to ensure that in Britain's schools Christian values and traditions be imparted. Education had its foundations in the monastery, the cathedral schools and the Board schools, which were also based very much on the church school model. Britain had inherited a Christian culture, and its education system and the laws of the land have drawn heavily upon biblical teaching and influence.[23]

While this may well have been the original intention, the cultural map has changed and a Christian culture cannot be relied upon as a foundation and mission mandate in today's context. Some of those advocating most vociferously that schools should comply with their duty to have Christianity as the predominant faith backdrop are also those who would oppose teaching other faiths and religions in our schools. While this viewpoint is perfectly understandable, it is firmly rooted in Christendom thinking. In the postmodern and post-Christendom era, Christianity is not and will not be a majority-held world view. In some schools in some parts of the UK it will be pushed (and is being pushed) so far to the margins that it will soon cease to register on the radar.

In future, those engaged in schools work need to be aware that the fixed and privileged positions of the past have been replaced by the multiple-choice worlds of pluralism and global diversity. The mindset that Christianity can be taught in schools from a premise of statuary control needs to be replaced by a commitment to embodying Christianity as a living faith.

Colonial Youth Work?

> We're gonna take this land for Jesus.

> *A definition*: 'colonialism' – forced change in which one culture, society, or nation dominates another.

One of the legacies of the Christendom disposition has been a colonizing approach to mission. From the days of Constantine and the Roman Empire through to the Crusades and, more lately, the rise of the neo-conservative agendas of right-wing churches in the USA and the UK, colonial mission has been seen in terms of converting the heathen, taming the savage, educating the uneducated and imposing social and political systems.

When we speak of 'colonialism' here, we are not seeking to question the importance of mission or of communicating and teaching Christian beliefs and values, which continue to be a key part of the calling and responsibility of the post-Christendom church, but we are seeking to explore the abuse of power and the cultural imposition that has so often accompanied the preaching of the gospel. Though colonialism was often portrayed as mission and 'taking land for Jesus', throughout the Christendom era it was characterized by the use of force to impose Christianity and so-called Christian morality on people with little regard to their personal freedoms.

Sometimes the colonial approach was subtle, but nonetheless it was dishonouring to those it sought to reach. The spread of youth work movements from England to Wales illustrates this aptly. At the turn of the nineteenth century, the Girls' Friendly Society, the Boy Scouts Association and Girl Guides began work in Wales. These organizations worked in the English language and were affiliated to the Anglican Church whereas those they sought to work with often spoke Welsh and worshipped at non-conformist churches.[24]

The legacy of the indoctrinating and enforcing approaches prevalent within the Christendom era can be seen in some of the models and trends that characterize sectors of the church today. Thus, those who were colonized in the Christendom era not only received the Christian message but also an enforced realignment of their values and traditions. Liberation theologians allude to a kind of muddle that has evolved in which the message (the gospel) has been confused with the model (how we do church) and a whole set of behaviours has been subliminally and less subliminally foisted on unsuspecting converts. We are reminded by Frost and Hirsch that such approaches contrast sharply with the incarnational ministry that many aspire to: 'The great danger in failing to practice mission incarnationally is cultural imperialism.'[25] In youth work terms this is very destructive as can be illustrated by the following story from a youth mission.

The mission week had been an all-singing, all-dancing affair in local schools, with drama groups, pop bands, dry ice, lights, dancing girls and loads of detached youth work and other activities. It had successfully engaged lots of young people who had no previous experience of Christianity.

The week ended with an event in a church building rather than in the marquee that had hosted most of the week's other activities. This event was in essence a church service and the minister in charge of the church structured it on the pattern of a normal church service, declaring that young people 'will have to get used to it if they are to join the church'.

Up to that point, the young people had engaged with bright lights and big promises; they had responded with enthusiasm and built good relationships. Now they were being offered a choice: to conform to how the church did things or basically not to bother. Not surprisingly, they didn't bother.

Attempts to colonize these young people failed. The reality of having the land taken for Jesus was not the attractive, challenging, life-giving and life-enhancing experience it should have been but exploitation, undelivered promises and disappointment. Christian mission, teaching and discipleship were very important in this church, but not to the extent of abandoning their cultural models.

Some current agendas and trends within Christian youth work smack of colonial approaches. Although they are not all a direct result of Christendom, some of the vestiges of the legacy mentioned earlier can be glimpsed. For example, when youth workers:

- insist that they know best;
- promote (both intentionally and unintentionally) a euro-centric view of God and theology;
- are restricted by structures that mean that mission and other attempts to build the kingdom, rather than being undertaken spontaneously by the young people, have to go through extensive leadership ratification – a paternalistic system that is not empowering and maintains dependence and centralized control;
- present negative and stereotypical views of other faith groups, views that are often ill-informed and are certainly not based upon experience (for example: Do workers challenge the media and political association of Islam with violence while ignoring the fact that many in the world associate Christianity with war and violence?);
- maintain hierarchical approaches to leadership (exemplified by 'promoting' some young people to be worship leaders, Bible teachers, etc., implying that they are more important than other young people);
- 'asset-strip' the skills and abilities of some young people and import these into the adult church settings while not allowing other young people with different skills, abilities and perspectives (that don't fit the adult agenda) to participate;

- fail to consistently challenge the negative forces in globalization and capitalism that merely endorse the continued marginalization and demonization of those who might be on the edge – including young people.

We have also heard many stories about how this colonial approach has resulted in some youth workers 'asset-stripping' other local youth work. Typically, this has involved a large church with significant youth provision drawing young people away from smaller churches. In one sense, there is nothing new in this phenomenon and any direct connections to Christendom are tenuous, to say the least – in fact, this trend is just as likely to reflect the consumer mentality prevalent within society. However, it is an interesting issue to consider in the light of the legacy left by colonialism.

Young people have a natural desire to be with others and to be involved in something that has a buzz and vibrancy about it. Indeed, many of the churches and organizations that are drawing in young people from other churches would argue that this is done in the interests of the young people themselves since they are being offered a wider range of activities and opportunities to meet with other young people. But the reality is that larger groups grow and smaller ones lose the few young people they had. While numbers and critical mass are important, so is a theology and youth work practice that can be contextualized and outworked with two or three young people as well as twenty or thirty plus.

In declaring that 'mega-churches will continue to acquire the best talent from the current crop of experimental churches', Andy Crouch reminds us that even pioneer youth work can fall victim to this scenario. We ourselves have seen youth projects begin in a locality only for the young people to be whisked off to a bigger church context as soon as they express an interest in Christianity. Smaller local communities are thereby plundered of mission and the young people themselves put at risk of developing a consumer approach to faith that will stay with them for life and erode any sense of doing mission. Taking the best talent and resources from colonial empires did not happen only in days gone by.

Once local communities have been deprived of their expression of Christian youth work, restoration is difficult. The accelerators for continued marginalization, isolation and loss of a Christian presence in a community are all in place. The fate of corner shops and community post offices and the rise of the supermarket should serve as a warning. The 'Tescoization' of Christian youth work is a very real threat to its existence in isolated, deprived or marginalized communities.

Summer Festivals

Conversations with young people suggest that for many the summer Christian festivals play an essential role in sustaining their faith. These mega events are designed to inspire, motivate and encourage young people. Many say that coming together with thousands of their peers generates excitement and a sense that God is on the move. Many feel it is the only time they can truly be themselves and express their faith in a lively and culturally appropriate way. Some find the festivals a spur to further action, growth, mission and kingdom-building.

However, for other young people these festivals have virtually no relevance to their daily walk with God. The highs of the lazy days of summer are often quickly forgotten in the business of life, the demands of the culture, the dryness of the local church and the hostility of the school environment. After festival-goers had returned from their summer experience, one person reflected, 'I knew it had been a good festival as people were high for two weeks after rather than the normal one.' This was not said with any cynicism but as a genuine evaluation, endorsement and appreciation of the summer event. While two weeks of 'going for God' might be better than none, the question remains as to what impact such events have upon young people and their discipleship walk.

One conversation with Kelly, a university student, was very revealing. While she had enjoyed and valued these festivals in her teenage years, she had subsequently come to reflect more ambivalently on their impact:

When I look back, I feel a bit manipulated. In the way it is set up. No one sees it as successful unless 80 per cent of the people fall over or something. You are under pressure to be spiritual. They have their place, but they are over-emphasized. It is something to fall back on and get re-charged for the next six months or whatever. Then you fall away. They should be something to enhance your relationship with God, not something that you rely upon for it.

At these events the consumer is king and consumer choice is about personal satisfaction and immediacy, traits that are often, if not always, in conflict with kingdom values. The answer to this predicament is, as one commentator stated, to 'stop giving consumers anything to consume. They need to participate!'[26]

As well as reflecting the consumerism of broader culture, summer festivals also give glimpses of aspects of the Christendom legacy, for instance, in the use of an up-front, monologue preaching style rather than dialogue. Stuart Murray identifies the vestiges of Christendom in performance-oriented services and the 'tendency of the short-lived multi-voiced developments to revert to the default mono-voiced position'.[27] The summer festivals appear to exemplify such approaches, which are then often taken wholesale and applied in smaller church-based contexts.

At present the summer festivals appear to be at the centre of the faith of many young people. Some report that they live for such events. One young person commented that if he could just get to the festival in August then everything would be okay. He could get right with God and go from there. This young person has now turned his back on God (hopefully, temporarily) and become immersed in the world of drugs.

To make matters worse, conversations with young people suggest that some of them have faked the spiritual experiences they have attributed to God. This is sad and epitomizes so much about current experiential culture, church expectations and the bankruptcy of Christendom ideals. Redemption and remedy for the discouragement that comes from hearing such stories can only be found in listening to the very many genuine and positive experiences young people have had.

A challenge to these events is that they are only sustainable while the cohort to make them financially viable exists – a huge

consideration given the marketing and branding clout and profile of the festivals. As we drift farther into an era of post-
Christendom and mission on the margins, a declining church
threatens this cohort and demands an alternative strategy. We
could argue that these events are symbolic of the end of
Christendom – a kind of farewell party for the Christendom era
– rather than huge successes, models for ecclesiology and potential strategies for revival.

Closing Thoughts

This chapter has largely explored the negative impacts that
Christendom has had upon Christian youth work. There are
some potentially positive impacts, such as the resources that
come from the Christendom legacy. These resources may be
physical, such as money and buildings, but also encapsulate the
heritage of learning that arises from past missionary endeavours
and the experience this provides for youth workers engaging
with young people post-Christendom. Inevitably, Christian tradition includes much from the Christendom era. It is a challenging
task to find within Christian tradition those elements that have
value and worth for youth work post-Christendom, but that are
unfettered by the values, norms and assumptions of the
Christendom perspective.

There are some who see the influence of Christendom as something to be grateful for. There is no doubt that the work of
Constantine in giving Christianity legal status provided the relatively fledgling faith with stability and profile. Had this not happened, Christianity might have 'remained forever a small and
obscure minority sect'.[28] In legalizing and formalizing Christianity, however, Constantine robbed it of its underground nature
and revolutionary component. He moved faith off the streets,
detached it from its association with the poor and marginalized
and drew it into the courts and palaces of the rich and powerful.

We have already touched upon the fact that many young
people struggle to tell their peers that they are Christians. As well
as being one of the failures of Christendom – in that there
was reliance upon the institution to do mission instead of the

individual – this is also a forerunner of the challenges of post-Christendom. Conversations with young people reveal that very few have a missional perspective towards their friends and peers. While understandable, given the hostility of the culture, this is alarming.

We are left wondering what happened to Eutychus. Did he become a missionary to his peers? Was his life changed forever by what happened to him or did he simply carry on as usual? Was he rolled out to tell his story every time there was an outreach event or did that sort of thing not happen then? We may never know, but such questions might provide further food for reflection.

The good news is that some excellent work is being done with young people that is ground-breaking, innovative and reflective of the church as a marginal mission movement rather than an institution. Youth work often paves the way for other ministries. In the areas of worship, outreach, discipleship, social action and general mobilization for mission, it has been young people and work with them that has often pioneered work and strategies subsequently embraced by 'adult church'. We should welcome these developments as we seek to avoid many other young people falling asleep in the course of learning about God and the hope he promises.

3

Perspectives on Young People, Life and Spirituality

It was a pleasure recently to meet a man in his eighties who had been working with young people for several decades. Perhaps what was most astonishing was that he, his daughter and his granddaughter all worked with young people in the same youth club. He could no doubt tell many stories and provide numerous illustrations to show how work with young people has changed over the years: the historical and wider cultural context of work with young people provide us with a great deal to explore and reflect upon.

Before examining missional responses to the legacy of the past and cultural nuances of current work with young people, it would seem appropriate to examine the world young people live in today, the position they find themselves in, the advantages and challenges of being a young person and some of the impact the world has had upon them in the twenty-first century.

Recently, in a letter to *The Daily Telegraph*, 110 teachers, psychologists, children's authors and other experts appealed to the government and others to act concerning what was happening to children and young people in the nation. The letter stated that

> children still need what developing human beings have always needed, including real food (as opposed to processed 'junk'), real play (as opposed to sedentary, screen-based entertainment), first-hand experience of the world they live in and regular interaction with the real-life significant adults in their lives.

They also need time. In a fast-moving hyper-competitive culture, today's children are expected to cope with an ever-earlier start to formal schoolwork and an overly academic test-driven primary curriculum. They are pushed by market forces to act and dress like mini-adults and exposed via the electronic media to material which would have been considered unsuitable for children even in the very recent past.

Our society rightly takes great pains to protect children from physical harm, but seems to have lost sight of their emotional and social needs. However, it's now clear that the mental health of an unacceptable number of children is being unnecessarily compromised, and that this is almost certainly a key factor in the rise of substance abuse, violence and self-harm among our young people.[1]

It is against this social backdrop that this chapter seeks to explore the world that young people live in. We do not intend to look in detail at specific youth subcultures or current trends and fads, which tend to be short-lived in their nature and influence, but instead will focus attention upon the big picture encompassing young people's lives and experience. Space only allows some snapshot perspectives, detailed analysis of the issues raised being beyond the scope of this book. If we are to work effectively and appropriately in the world of young people, however, it is important to understand that world and to be able to take into account and appraise cultural contexts, situations and perspectives.

Some aspects of the human condition are undoubtedly timeless. Hence, some issues relating to young people have been consistent throughout history. These would include issues such as pushing boundaries, handling family, peer and intimate relationships, wrestling with parental demands and experiencing hormonal changes. But equally, some particular issues that have risen to the fore in this postmodern and post-Christendom era appear to have added significance at this time. It is on these that we focus here.

Respect

Perhaps one word above all others has dominated many recent conversations with adult members of the public about young people – the word 'respect'. Adults consistently comment that young people no longer have any respect for people, property, their elders, society and just about anything else. Over 80 per cent of adults think that young people do not have enough respect for traditional British values.[2] The truth of this perception is open to question, but it is nevertheless a driver behind many social and political responses to young people. The outcome of such a view-point is that at almost every opportunity, young people are demonized by the media and politicians, while members of local communities are quick to blame them for many of society's ills. The myth that young people are the root of all evil is sadly popular. A recent survey among young people found that:

- 98 per cent of young people felt the media always, often or sometimes represented them as anti-social;
- fewer than 10 per cent of young people felt they had done more than two things that were anti-social in the last 12 months;
- over 80 per cent felt they were represented by the media as a group to be feared;
- 86 per cent felt they were seldom or never portrayed as a group to be trusted;
- 75 per cent lose respect for politicians when they say negative things about young people;
- more than 90 per cent do not believe that politicians treat them as equals;
- they would like to tell adults that what problems there are occur because of a very small minority of young people.[3]

Respect needs to be a two-way process. It is not just about young people respecting adults. It is also about adults respecting young people and when this is absent, the consequences will continue to be that young people are demonized. Such an outcome may well lead to young people fulfilling the negative impression people have of them. Society gets the teenagers it deserves. They are a product of their adult parents, mentors, politicians, media representatives and youth workers! Tim Evans, Chief Executive of Worth Unlimited, reminds us that we are all in this together:

Some young people, down to some combination of circumstances and choice, do things they shouldn't and need to take responsibility for their actions. But firstly, we all need to take responsibility for the broken society, what we would call a 'non Shalom society', that is a causal factor in which we are all complicit and have a degree of responsibility.[4]

The church has an opportunity to model something different and to value young people by giving them the respect and dignity they deserve as part of God's creation. If it refuses to look down on young people simply because they are young (1 Tim. 4:12), then it might be that they in their turn will show themselves to be good citizens and, hopefully, faithful believers.

Achievements

Matt was recently disappointed when he only got two As and a B at 'A' level. Though these results are fantastic, both he and his parents were devastated that he didn't obtain the grades he needed to get into his first-choice university. Such experiences have become commonplace for many young people. Educational standards have risen and higher and higher grades are being achieved. But young people often feel discouraged because rather than celebrating such achievements, people are suggesting that the exams have got easier!

We now have 3-years-olds who can use a personal computer. And there are very many young people who take a gap year to develop their skills and serve others, or volunteer in a wide variety of community-based projects, or take part in sports and physical activity on a regular basis, or are the main carers for siblings or disabled parents. Such achievements are significant and worthy of recognition and celebration.

While perhaps overstating the case for the cultural changes that have taken place, Deirdre Fernand offers a view that contrasts sharply with that often presented by the media:

Teenagers, they're not what they used to be. Once you could rely upon them to be surly slug-a-beds, not rising to noon, filling their bedrooms with smelly socks and your house with studied silences. But no, here they are, sailing solo across oceans, trekking across ice floes and clinging onto sheer rock faces, all the while being bright, charming and even remembering to take their homework with them as they scale the giddy heights of achievement.[5]

Even those young people who might be deemed socially excluded seem to be achieving more than their predecessors. Many are highly enterprising, creative and full of energy, embracing the arts, technology and, very often, difficult life situations to make the most of the opportunities they have. Youth workers need to throw more parties to mark such achievements and take advantage of the many schemes that exist to accredit young people's endeavours and achievements.

Behaviour

Sadly, we hear more about young people's bad behaviour than their good achievements. Virtually every media report informs us of how bad young people are, with reports of challenging behaviour, anti-social behaviour orders, drug and alcohol abuse and statistics showing the increasing incidence of sexual diseases. On the television, we repeatedly see the same video clip of some young people breaking into a van. This clip is used almost like an advertisement. Such denigration is a form of discrimination and wouldn't be tolerated against any other section of society.

It may well be true that in some respects young people's behaviour is worse than that of their predecessors. There is no doubt that sexually transmitted infections have increased markedly and incidents of binge drinking have multiplied significantly in recent years. However, these increases have also been experienced by adults in their thirties and are by no means exclusively young people's problems. The fear of crime by young people is greater than the incidence of crime, which has fallen quite dramatically in recent years. Fear of young people, and, consequently, resentment of them, are higher in the UK than in any other European country.[6]

Perhaps those young people who are badly behaved have simply copied the politicians, media and big-business moguls who are so quick to condemn them. As Francis Gilbert suggests, from time to time all of these people use bullying techniques, abuse their power and positions of responsibility and set very poor standards for the rest of society.[7] Numerous scandals, resignations, accusations, counter-accusations and public enquiries provide ample evidence of anti-social behaviour at this level of society.

We would also do well to remember that young people are more often the victims than the perpetrators of crime. In 2003, 5,570 young people aged 10 to 24 were murdered in the United States, and 82 per cent of these were killed with firearms.[8] Stabbings and shootings of young people are on the increase in the UK with many recent high-profile cases attracting considerable media attention.

While others attack young people and bring sanctions against them to control their behaviour, perhaps the Christian community would be better served by addressing the question of why young people and young adults engage in such behaviour. Only by looking at the causes from a kingdom perspective will we make progress on these issues. Constantly bemoaning the actions of young people will do nothing to help solve the problems. Asking the 'Why?' questions is essential if we are to give effective help.

Health

Today's young people are likely to live longer than any other generation before them. At the same time, they are increasingly suffering from obesity, poor mental health and allergy-based illnesses.

The hours spent on the internet and on computer games and young people's increasing tendency to undertake activities on their own in their own bedrooms have all contributed to their gaining weight.[9] This, coupled with a shortage of places to play and do sport (because we have built houses on the playing fields and banned ball games in many areas) and an addiction to fast food (often increased by a generation of parents who can't or won't cook and provide a balanced diet) have created the most obese generation of young people yet. Research suggests that up to a third of young people in the UK are overweight or obese with the figure repeatedly rising in recent years.[10] The National Health and Nutrition Examination Survey suggests that 16 per cent of children and adolescents in the United States are obese.[11] Canadian obesity rates trebled between 1985 and 2000 and one quarter of Canadian children are now considered obese.[12]

Mental health is perhaps the greatest cause for concern today, with young people suffering from a variety of emotional, conduct and hyperkinetic (activity) disorders. Estimates vary, but some reports suggest that at some point or other in their childhood or adolescence, up to 30 per cent of young people in the UK, and 10 per cent at any one time, suffer from one of these conditions.[13] Of young people in prison, nine out of ten have mental health issues.[14]

Eating disorders continue to be a major illness for some young people and incidents of self-harm are on the increase.[15] Suicide remains one of the major causes of death among this age range and, according to the Samaritans, is the most common cause of death, after accidents, in young men aged between 15 and 24.

Such facts about the state of mental health of young people are an appalling indictment upon society and again the question as to why this should be comes to the fore. Perhaps mental health is tied to spiritual health, and poor mental health is another symptom of spiritual impoverishment. Churches need to view mental health issues as they view other medical problems and respond appropriately with prayer, spiritual warfare and compassionate support.

Expectations

The postmodern era is characterized by a vast array of choices encompassing almost all aspects of western society. It is equally marked by an individualistic approach to life. This has engendered huge expectations. Young people both aspire to achieving such expectations, and are the victims of the expectations of others.

Reference has already been made to educational achievements. The expectation is that all young people will achieve academically. This brings huge pressures, especially for those young people who are not naturally gifted in this area or who have not learned to play the system. Parents and youth workers need to caution themselves before jumping on the middle-class 'university education for all' bandwagon, which is clearly not in the best interests of all young people. The overarching goal is surely to enable young people to be released into the plan and purpose that God has for them, not to pigeon-hole them into a single way of living their lives.

Sadly, the consumer society puts significant pressure upon parents as well as young people. The quest for ever more expensive houses, designer goods and the latest gadgets has caused huge amounts of personal consumer debt, which many struggle to live with. In the attempt to manage such commitments, parents come under pressure to work longer hours; inevitably something has to give and too often it is the parenting of young people that suffers. It is a modern paradox that parenting skills have been much emphasized and have come under intense scrutiny in the very culture in which many children are child-minded when they are young, and then coerced into attending after-school activities. By the time they are teenagers young people are often spending ten or more hours a day at school. Exactly when any parenting might take place is open to question.

Speaking on BBC radio, the award-winning children's author Michael Morpurgo attributed young people's mental health problems, sleep and eating disorders to their being packed off to school at too early an age rather than being nurtured in the family. His view that lack of contact between parents and their children is directly to blame might be overstated but it should not be dismissed at a time when pressure on young people is so high and growing.

As if these factors were not harmful enough, young people also have to cope with pressure and high expectations from their peers, churches or other faith bodies (if they attend), parents, possibly stepparents, and sports or other interest groups. If we are not careful, these expectations will compound the health issues and push young people over the edge.

Opportunities

Perhaps one of the reasons why churches have failed to attract and keep young people in recent times is that there are simply so many opportunities to do other things that are perceived as more attractive and entertaining (noting that the objective of church is not to pander to consumer demands to be entertained). Back in 2002, Peter Brierley's research established that the main reason why tweenagers didn't go to church, or stopped going, was down to a perception of boredom (87 per cent) with 67 per cent simply saying that they had other things to do on a Sunday.[16]

Young people can access and undertake international travel like no generation before them and will consequently experience more diverse and exciting cultures and experiences. Technology has given access to communication tools that are immediate and available 24/7. Mobile phones, the internet and video technologies have built new communities for young people to be part of. Some adults tend to belittle such communities as not being 'real' because they don't entail face-to-face contact. Such a view is erroneous and runs the risk of further alienating those young people who live in, for and by such communities. We will examine this in more detail shortly.

For those young people so motivated, there is a vast array of gap-year schemes, local initiatives and national programmes, which offer opportunities to serve as volunteers both locally and further afield. Possibilities exist for young people to serve on decision-making bodies, consultative groups, the youth parliament, school councils and other bodies where their views are taken seriously and where they are encouraged to take responsibility for the areas of life that affect them. While progress has been made, the church has been slow to involve young people in decision-making processes.[17] It is to be hoped that this change will gather momentum as the post-Christendom church becomes less an institution and more a grass-roots, bottom-up movement that takes account of everyone's views in a more deliberate way.

Religion and Spirituality

The end of Christendom has dealt a confusing blow to those seeking to understand young people's spirituality. During the height of this era, there was a degree of certainty about how young people 'did' spirituality and there were clearly identifiable patterns of faith development with children probably going to Sunday school and then progressing on to youth groups and clubs before moving into 'adult' church. As the Christendom era has drawn to a close, this process only takes place with a very small minority of young people. Faith and spiritual development have become elusive constructs and abstract notions, and the post-Christendom era has become synonymous with clouded spiritual parameters. This has led to a plethora of research studies that all attempt to provide clearer pictures about what might be going on in the spiritual lives of young people.[18] The conclusions reached by this research have not always had the desired clarity, which is perhaps confirmation in itself that we are moving away from a clear Christendom paradigm to something less precise, quantifiable and coherent.

Walter Brueggemann has done extensive studies of the Psalms and has helpfully suggested that they fall into three overarching categories, which speak of 'orientation', 'disorientation' and 'reorientation'.[19]

- Orientation psalms talk of everything being ordered and right in the world. Everything makes sense and life is not threatened or troubled. We know who God is and where he can be found. For example, Psalms 8, 37, 111.
- Disorientation psalms remind us of storms and discontent in life, which cause us to feel that we are stuck in a pit. We are often unwilling to admit to these problems and frequently seek to dismiss them, which ultimately compounds our problems. God is often hard to find and we can feel abandoned. For example, Psalms 13, 51, 143.
- Reorientation psalms speak of the joy and thanksgiving that arise as we are delivered from the pit of despair. We easily recognize God's grace in our lives. For example, Psalms 23, 66, 103.

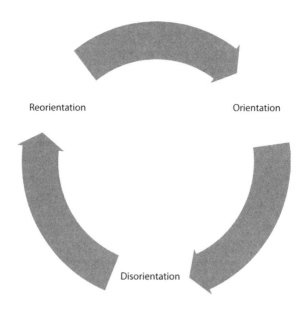

Reorientation   Orientation

Disorientation

Brueggemann's analysis of the Psalms

Such an analysis can be adapted and applied to our current spiritual culture. Christendom might be viewed as a time of orientation.
In the Christendom era most people knew that western society was
modelled upon Christian principles; moral and ethical frameworks
were permeated with Christendom thinking; the days of the week
and our calendars were structured around Christian teachings and
festivals; and work with young people was based on the assumption that they lived in a Christian country and paradigm.[20]

In the last few decades, this orientation has been threatened
and eroded dramatically, resulting in a 'disorientated' view of the
Christian faith, in particular, and the spiritual, in general. It could
be suggested that as we approach the end of the Christendom
era, the church has generally not sought to engage with the idea
of being disorientated, preferring instead the comfort of assum-
ing that everything is all right. The suggestion is that this denial
has actually caused an acceleration of the demise of Christendom
and compounded the many challenges that relate to work with
young people.

The advent of a post-Christendom era combined with a post-modern perspective has, in effect, disorientated our understanding and perceptions. We have moved from seeing spirituality as exclusively or even mainly 'Christian' to not being sure what spirituality is all about. This has ensured that debates about spirituality are shrouded in mystery and a lack of clarity. To some extent, this is inevitable given the nature of the subject, but it has not helped the work of exploring spirituality with young people.[21]

What is clear, however, is that what were once spiritual 'givens' are now distant memories. The new world of spiritual disorientation has produced a plethora of relativistic beliefs, an abundance of spiritual choice and unfettered religious pluralism interwoven to an unprecedented extent with secular ideas. In the USA, young people in the 18- to 25- year-old range believe in religious diversity and when asked about what concerns them, list, above the issue of God and religion, worries and challenges about sex, relationships, finding a good job and how to deal with the changing economy. Only 7 per cent of the young people surveyed said that their friends came exclusively from the same religion.[22]

For the Christendom Christian, such a season of disorientation can be threatening. It is an 'in-between' period of transition from the certainties of how things used to be to the uncertainty of how things are and the dream of how things might be once reorientation has been achieved. This may take a long time.

The following table illustrates one model of learning that can help our exploration.[23]

Stages of learning

Stages of learning	What it feels like
Unconscious incompetence	You do not know what you do not know
Conscious incompetence	You know what you do not know, and you may not like it
Conscious competence	You know what you know and practising the new skill or

	knowledge may feel rather clumsy
· Unconscious competence	You feel as if you have always known what you know, as it comes naturally

It might be said that at the end of the Christendom era we were unconsciously incompetent in relation to our Christian faith. Although many Christians felt confident and secure, Christianity was often simply part of a cultural package rather than a living, vibrant faith. The emergence of post-Christendom has now called into question many of our assumptions and has challenged our complacency.

As denominations, networks and individual churches face the reality of decline, the subsequent questioning, analysis and reflection can leave us feeling that we actually have more questions than answers and this sets us firmly in the place of conscious incompetence. In this regard the model above is an encouragement. The movement from unconscious to conscious incompetence is actually a significant move forward and helps us begin a learning journey to gain the fresh skills and knowledge needed for the new context.

It may be said that many young people do not know what they do not know about Christianity. Such a view is supported by their spiritual illiteracy, their confusion over who is who in biblical stories, their jumbled ideas about the beliefs of different faiths, and lifestyle choices that are based upon 'feel-good' factors rather than faith-based meta-narratives. Many simply appear no longer to have the words to describe, connect or contextualise any spiritual experiences they might have. Rankin goes further when he states that young people 'have the most profound thoughts and feelings about a spiritual world . . . yet they struggle to consider themselves spiritual or express with any confidence their understanding of terms such as spiritual, spirituality or spiritual experience'.[24] In essence, young people are increasingly becoming, or have already become, 'incompetent' in this regard.

Other Faith Groups

While the position relating to religion and spirituality might be complex, it is also clear that increasing numbers of young people practise faiths other than Christianity. In the UK, these are largely the children of first, second and now third generation immigrants. Many have very real faith experiences, albeit to varying degrees. This presents some specific challenges for youth workers, who often have little experience of working with such young people. Andrew Smith challenges British youth workers in this regard:

> Living among other faiths raises big issues because much of our youth work philosophy assumes that the non-Christians we work with are secular, and live highly individualistic lives. So what then might mission look like for young people committed to their own faith? (Should we even contemplate mission among young people of other faiths?) How do we help young people make choices when the opinions of their family will have a huge influence on them?[25]

Such a cultural dynamic cannot be ignored and it is further evidence that we are moving to a pluralist culture in which the church has lost its privileged position. At the same time, young people from other faith backgrounds might also be experiencing the same dynamic of pluralism. Christianity is not the only faith to be influenced by secularism, materialism and disparaging views of young people. While we would argue that many Christian young people are living with the consequences of a post-Christendom paradigm, there is some evidence that this position is not unique to Christianity. There is a strong case for arguing that young people generally are living in an increasingly 'post-faith' culture as traditional values, community principles and practices are eroded.

> The tie between culture and faith is significant in many other faith groups and is much more clearly identified than in Christian circles. Celebrations, communities, families, festivals and activities are often intrinsically linked to traditional faith and beliefs. Faith leaders have strong influences over many communities. There

does, however, appear to be some tensions developing around these issues.

Over the last forty years the Christian Church has experienced a large exodus by young people. It could well be that this process is underway in other faith communities . . . youth workers . . . indicate that young people from other faith backgrounds are increasingly turning their backs on their traditional faith. For example, in some cases, Muslim leaders are asking questions as to why the young people are no longer going to prayers at the mosque. Some have stated that they do not believe that community and faith leaders will allow this to happen on the scale seen by the Christian Church while others have stated that it is already underway and will be impossible to stop. A Muslim elder said that, 'If Muslims were wise, they would look at what has happened to the Christian church.'[26]

We therefore find ourselves in an even more complex situation where we not only have young people who have no faith, we have those who have an active faith and those who have what we might term a cultural heritage-based faith, which is on the wane. This level of diversity needs to be understood if mission with young people is to be undertaken effectively.

View from the Margins

The introduction to the *Breakdown Britain* report reminds us that

> the welfare society has been breaking down on the margins, and the social fabric of many communities is being stripped away. Although this has been increasingly accepted by commentators and academics in recent years, a defensive complacency, akin to attitudes towards Britain's industrial decline in the 1970s, has characterised our reaction to this problem. Too many either do not care or feel powerlessness to do anything about it. This study starkly illustrates the deleterious effect this breakdown is having on our children.[27]

While it is true that many young people achieve great things, have unparalleled opportunities and great expectations, there remains a significant minority to whom this does not apply. They are those young people who remain socially excluded, living in disadvantage and poverty.

Fortunately, the church has begun to respond to this group with a host of social action and community projects. Much more needs to be done, however, if we are to avoid a large section of society becoming totally alienated from the rest of the community. The journalist Jane Shilling sums this up eloquently when she says, 'It is a curious view of the world that sees in groups of children not a fund of pleasure and hope for the future, but a source of alarm and distress to local communities. To treat any minority as apart from society is to invite them to become so.' Distinctive skills are required in working with this cohort of young people and the challenges should not be underestimated.

When we add the context of a fast-moving world that is driven by the knowledge economy,[29] then we see that socially excluded young people are conspired against even further. In the past, such a cohort often had the security of knowing that they would have a job in a manufacturing-based industry where they might work for the rest of their lives. The modern global economy no longer affords such securities. The new knowledge economy requires technology, information and communication skills, human resources aptitudes, service provision capacities and soft, interpersonal skills. Sadly, these are often the very skills that this cohort of young people most lack. They risk becoming still further entrenched in their social exclusion if they do not access this new world and acquire the appropriate skills. Experience in recent times has suggested that efforts to bring about these changes are not very effective.

Hope

The above illustrations hopefully present some snapshots of what is happening to young people at the present time. They reveal a strange mixture of struggle, pain and potentially destructive processes working tangentially alongside tremendous endeavour, potential, resilience and hope.

In the New Testament, Paul reminds us that faith, hope and love are eternal attributes of the kingdom and will remain even when everything else has been removed (1 Cor. 13:13). We talk a lot about love and faith; hope seems to be the poor relation. Paul is writing about the hope of God – the future (and present) reality of the kingdom of heaven. Life without hope is a difficult thing.

Often youth workers can slip into the mentality of thinking that it is they and they alone who bring hope to young people. This can be especially true if they tie hope in with a message about God and the hope that he brings. While there is some truth in this way of thinking, it is interesting to consider the hope that young people themselves bring – not because of any particular success or achievement, but simply because they are young.

Many conversations with young people, individually and in groups, reveal that what is most important to them is their friends and family. These relationships provide young people with their key experiences of belonging and community, and appear to be crucial to their welfare. It is into and out of these relationships that hope often springs. Having the security of stable friends and family remains a key determinant in young people's futures.

Reflecting on many years' experience of working with young people, Tim Evans reminds us of their capacity to overcome apparently overwhelming difficulties when he says: '[I have] met and heard stories about young people who have redeemed their lives and, far from being the once bad always bad stereotype, have found ways to change and become positive people living positive lives.'[30]

When we hear stories of the difficult situations in which many young people live, we find it truly amazing that they carry on at all. Many exemplify hope for the future in the way they deal with the challenges of life: the girl who, as a teenager, tragically loses both her parents, but goes on to complete her education and progress to university; the young carer who looks after his severely disabled mum; the 16-year-old girl suffering from anorexia and near death who by the age of 19 has recovered to travel the world and continue her education; the girl with ME who goes to serve as a missionary in Africa. This list could go on and on. Such expressions of hope embody the human spirit and provide a glimpse of the endurance, creativity, capacity and potential that is present within God's creation.

If youth workers are to play their part in helping young people fulfil the hope they bring, then anything they can do must be considered a privilege not to be belittled. Hope can become infectious and the hopefulness of youth can rub off on others of a more mature age. Anecdotal evidence is suggesting that those young people who currently have a passion for Christianity are unfazed by the challenges of post-Christendom. They are blissfully unaware of the potential demise of the church and only see the future as positive. Whether this is denial fuelled by over-enthusiastic adult mentors or a genuine faith that God is on the move is open to debate, but the fact remains that they are full of hope and expectation.

What Are the 'Whys'?

It's very easy to identify what might be wrong with society and in particular young people. There are many people doing this and making a living from it! However, the number of people asking *why* things are as they are is alarmingly low. Policies, services and reactions to young people seem to be predominantly focused on putting right 'wrongs' without ever addressing the question of what caused these wrongs in the first place. Such approaches are futile, a waste of money and demoralizing for youth workers, who are often pulled from pillar to post at the whim of a policy change or the latest initiative following a 'bad news' report about young people. If we are to serve young people effectively, we need to focus our energies and resources on the causes and not the symptoms of the problems and challenges they face. We need to ask, 'Why is it like this?'

Perhaps one answer to this question is that in recent times the Christendom church has concentrated on the issue of personal sin rather than corporate folly. Clearly they are interlinked, but only by seeing the big picture of culture and society can we begin to address the challenges effectively. The following quotations show the malaise in which substantial sections of society and young people find themselves:

> Worryingly, a disproportionate number of those committing anti-social acts, becoming teenage parents and consuming drugs and

alcohol hail from lower socio-economic groups. Social mobility appears to have stalled: today Britain's young people's futures are more strongly determined by their backgrounds and upbringing than was the case for previous generations.[31]

Family breakdowns, educational failure, economic dependence, indebtedness and addictions are all interrelated . . . Children from a broken home are twice as likely to have behavioural problems, become sexually active at a younger age, suffer depression and turn to drugs, smoking and heavy drinking.[32]

In my own experience, most of the young people who have caused harm to others, have done so because of a perceived injustice where they have been harmed first, creating a continual cycle of hurt and leaving an aftermath of hurt young people who lose faith in justice.[33]

Unless youth work takes into account the poverty in which many young people find themselves, we will not get very far. It continues to be the case that many of the youth workers who work with young people from poor communities end up changing their theology to meet the context they work in. The theology they had before has often been found wanting when faced with the challenges of poor housing, violence, gross injustice, addiction, debt and children who are often virtually un-parented.

A theology of the suburbs might be described as being typified by:

- learning by systematic study;
- worship that is about selecting from a rather narrow choice of styles and genres;
- perceiving and promoting a view of God who gives continual pleasant spiritual experiences;
- a church that entertains in the context of seeing faith as a market choice;
- promotion of good manners, behaviour, conformity and balance;
- valuing the individual, personal security, happiness and space;
- freedom from influences that prevent happiness.

In contrast, a theology of the marginalized might focus upon:

- learning from life;
- a quest for social justice;
- finding God in the struggle and dark places;
- promotion of shalom as an ideal;
- the significance of community;
- appreciating the corporate;
- liberation from oppression.

Family breakdown cannot be overlooked. It has an impact on the emotional and mental health of young people. Irrespective of whether or not a young person is socially excluded, the loss of a parental figure will cause pain and uncertainty, and threaten stability. When combined with poverty, poor housing, drug and/or alcohol abuse, parents not talking to their children and families never eating together, the consequences can be extremely damaging. When such patterns have become embedded in the lives and communities within which young people live, the results can be catastrophic and contribute to poor educational attainment, challenging behaviour and lack of aspirations.

When all these factors are set into the context of a culture obsessed with consumption, then problems are inevitable. The underlying issues of why people are poor, why they take drugs, why they abuse their children and why they have to consume so many things must be addressed if we are to progress and help remedy some of these challenges.

Perhaps the insecurities that exist because of the absence of a living faith and walk with God cause people to be fearful. Fear then makes them selfish and over-protective of what they have, and this in turn means that a culture emerges in which everyone seeks to protect their own interests, preserve their own positions and satisfy their own desires. We can see these kinds of patterns in the history book of Judges, where people ceased to follow God's ways and turned instead to doing their own thing, ending up in chaos. Sadly, for many young people this is the daily reality in which they live.

Reflections

We began this chapter by referring to a man who had been work-ing with young people for many decades. His passion, commit-ment, love and understanding of young people have not only kept him going but helped build many, many effective and fruit-ful relationships. Whatever the cultural changes that have taken place during his lifetime, these relationships have been the key.

We have tried to get to the heart of some of the cultural drivers that currently relate to young people. Jesus also got straight to the heart of the matter. Whenever he talked with people, he always put his finger on the key issues, the significant matters, the essen-tial barriers to life. He did this consistently, as we see in his encounters with individuals such as the Samaritan woman at the well (Jn. 4) and the rich young ruler (Mk. 10). Insight into rela-tionships with young people needs that same sensitivity to the Spirit.

We will explore methods of mission more fully shortly, but it is worth noting that Jesus got involved in the community, with people. He didn't keep his distance from the challenges but engaged and engaged effectively and consistently with those with whom he shared his life. He combined this with living life to the full, going to parties, weddings, social functions and cul-tural activities. It would be hoped that youth workers will simi-larly engage with people when addressing some of the challenges referred to above.

Equality, fairness and justice underpinned all that Jesus said and did. He told things how they were and was not afraid to con-front institutional sin. He showed respect to all, including children and women, who in Jewish society were frequently overlooked and looked down upon. The only people he had harsh words for were the pious religious leaders of the day. Again, perhaps this is a model for youth workers to take forward! These leaders were appalled at the behaviour of Jesus and his band of young disciples, who, if they were around today, would no doubt be served with dispersal orders, while Mary and Joseph would be criticized for their lack of parenting skills.

As well as enjoying the good times, Jesus also wept with those who were suffering, mourned with the bereaved and shared the pain of those in distress. We have looked at some of the challenges facing the marginalized. There are many opportunities to get alongside those young people who are struggling with life and facing stressful and uncertain futures. If a by-product of this coming alongside is that such young people are set free, then that would be a cause for rejoicing, but it would be hoped that the primary reason for being there was just that – being there.

Jesus was also familiar with the challenges of working in a spiritually demanding environment. He had the heritage of the Jewish faith, a faith that had become distorted over the centuries and was somewhat different from that proposed by God. He lived in a culture that was influenced by Hellenistic thinking and was at the mercy of the Roman imperialists. He was caught between the two dominant spiritual forces of Judaism and the Roman Empire, which ultimately cost him his life. We can continue to learn from his experience of working within the context of an oppressive, opposing and troubled society. Reading the gospels afresh with this uppermost in our minds brings new understanding and revelation about struggle and hope.

Be it sharing a meal with those no one liked (Mk. 2:15), stopping in the crowd when he was in a rush in order to heal a women ostracized by society (Mk. 5:21–34) or in the final throes of life encouraging a thief on a cross (Lk. 23:39–43), Jesus always had time for the individual. Young people need people who will look out for them, listen to them and take them seriously. Jesus did all of these things, modelling something all of us can aspire to.

4

Mission: Reaching Young People Post-Christendom

We move on from exploring the impact that Christendom has had upon youth work and young people, to considering some possible responses to the question of how we might undertake work and mission with young people in this new context. It is important to stress here that we are not seeking to discover how we can somehow preserve the Christendom approaches we have, but rather to suggest ways of approaching youth work and mission that are sustainable and appropriate to the post-Christendom reality of faith on the margins of society.

It is important to acknowledge from the outset that every context is different. Every church, group, community and team will need to consider their own situation in terms of the culture of the young people they are engaging with, their interests, needs and aspirations. It is also worth remembering that culture is not static. Today as never before the pace of change is significant and the ever-changing cultural environment in which we work will demand awareness and adaptation. Ridderstrale and Nordstrom, commenting on the uncertainties associated with the time in which we live, write:

> We see a gigantic spiritual vacuum. It is a mist sweeping over the world filling us with doubts and hesitation. We are no longer pilgrims with a clear mission living in a well-structured environment. Instead we have become wandering vagabonds in search of . . . ?[1]

The sentence is left incomplete, such is the writer's hesitation about what we are actually seeking. It is into this context that work with young people is undertaken and all the suggestions we make need to be contextualized into this constantly changing environment.

In the 2006 film *Superman Returns*, Superman says to his long-time love, Lois Lane, 'You wrote that the world doesn't need a saviour, but every day I hear the world crying out for one.' We start from a place of believing that, whether consciously or unconsciously, young people are on a journey in which they are trying to get to grips with all that is wrong in the world and are searching for meaning and purpose. In the midst of personal struggles, local issues and global uncertainty, they are open to finding meaning and purpose and the hope that the future may hold if only a saviour were forthcoming.

Integration

In considering issues of mission, we want to address first one of the most common questions asked by youth workers at the training sessions we run: 'How can we integrate non-Christian young people into the church?' This question comes in a variety of guises:

- How can you work with churched young people and non-churched young people?
- Now that we've done Youth Alpha, what's the best way of getting the young people who have done it along to Sunday services?
- How can the programmes we run work with those who want to study the Bible and those who want to just get together and be friends?
- How can we stop all the young people from Christian families leaving when the kids from the local estate come along?

While the question might be phrased in a variety of different ways, the heart of the issue is always the same. Having done some mission, the goal is to get the young people into what is already happening in the church. This approach smacks of a

Christendom mindset of the highest order. A huge amount of energy and enterprise is invested into trying to integrate young people into existing structures. Church services are tweaked, special events are devised, publicity is designed, and bribes – including food, special music events, prizes and competitions – are offered. Although these are usually all ineffective, the processes themselves can cause strife among existing congregations as old and young alike become discontented with what is perceived as pandering to young people outside the church.

Some older people don't like modern expressions of church, worship and activity, the parents of the Christian young people may want their offspring to undertake Bible study and prayer so that they grow up 'in the faith' and some young people are positively resistant to non-Christian young people joining their group as it was the only safe space they had in the first place. These factors can combine to conspire against any kind of integration ever happening.

The reality is that integration is not at all easy. It is hard enough for many adults who are unfamiliar with church culture to engage with church, but for young people outside the church, there are simply far too many cultural barriers to cross. The story of Eutychus again serves as a helpful illustration. He couldn't stay awake. The way the teaching was done was just too great a gulf for him to bridge and he got bored, switched off, fell asleep and shipped out.

There are some challenging stories of churches who have managed to make integration work and these must not be overlooked. One example is that of the Shal church in Grimsby where John Ellis has done amazing work in transforming church life, youth work and mission into a meaningful and well-developed expression of a local Christian community that is extremely well integrated into a marginalized working class community. It has to be acknowledged that this is largely due to John's long-term commitment to the area, his creative leadership and his imaginative and progressive approach to developing church and mission. At Shal, the structures and methodologies of church have been crafted to make them relevant to young people and adults who have no prior experience of Christianity and the focus is very much on building community rather than attending services. Our experience would suggest, however, that stories such as this are the exception rather than the norm.

Having asked questions about integration, many youth workers are shocked when the answer given is, 'Why try? If I were you, I wouldn't bother.' A host of theological justifications for integration come flying back. Isn't it important for the whole church community to worship together? What about the issue of church being family? How will young people learn if they don't come to church on a Sunday or attend Bible study?

The reality is that we are all one body, but many Christians don't regularly mix with people from other ethnic, social and economic groupings. Families can be close without enjoying the same TV programmes, music, social activities and friendship groups. So it can be with church and Christian youth work.

The Mission of God

> Mission is not primarily an activity of the church but an attribute of God. God is a missionary God . . . Mission is thereby seen as a movement from God to the world; the church is viewed as an instrument for that mission . . . There is church because there is mission, not vice versa.[2]

Understanding God's heart and passion for reaching people will significantly help us in our approaches to mission with young people. Rather than seeing mission primarily as something we have to do, it is much simpler, and much more authentic, to seek to identify how God is working among a particular group of young people and join in with this. From here we might then go on to see how an expression of church develops.[3] This idea of joining with the *missio dei* (mission of God) can be very liberating for youth workers as it brings with it the security of knowing that it really is God at work.

When we approach mission in this way, we do not need to force an agenda or conspire to get young people into church or to a special event. Instead, we open our eyes, listen to the voice of the Spirit and really begin to engage with the young people around us. In many ways, this is far more costly than simply putting on an event, but it carries the possibility of undertaking some truly exciting work. As Bonhoeffer reminds us, 'Every attempt to impose the gospel by force, to run after people and proselytize them, to use our own resources to arrange the salvation of other people, is both futile and dangerous'.[4] We would do well to embrace this reminder in our approaches to work with young people.

The following example of work being undertaken in Coventry illustrates the possibilities that exist when we join with God in mission, seek to see work emerge with a specific group of young people and free ourselves from the stresses of having to integrate a group into current work.

A group of 14- to 23-year-old Goths have traditionally hung around a church building in Coventry city centre. On one occasion some of them wandered into a church service, to be greeted by the church ushers who promptly gave them a pile of hymn books. When engaged in conversation, the Goths said that they were cold and thirsty. In fact, many of them were homeless and unemployed. Those within the church who were interested in working with young people sat and listened and over time began to develop ongoing relationships with them.

The Goths were invited to come along to the Christian youth group and some of them did this. The Christian young people in the group didn't really engage with them, were afraid of them and largely hid from them. In response to this lack of integration, the youth workers ran an *Alpha* course for the Goths but this was not a great success. The Goths liked the youth workers, enjoyed the club, but found that *Alpha* was asking questions that were simply not relevant to them. As a result, the workers ended up lecturing them on matters they didn't want to know about. The key issues facing them were not questions about the existence of God and discipleship, but rather more practical ones about finding jobs and somewhere to live.

Over time, the youth workers observed that the Goths were particularly into candles, incense and imagery. So they decided to use these particular dynamics to do something small that had a specifically Christian focus, and began a service modelled on Compline (Night Prayer), using a liturgy around a short Celtic prayer. This has proved very successful in drawing others in. At the time of writing, there are around 50 Goths involved with the youth workers.

To outside observers the work with the Goths in Coventry might appear tremendously significant, but much of the work is relational and although there is a definite spiritual aspect, this must not be overemphasized. In fact, most of the time the workers spend with the Goths is focused simply around informal conversation, with 'bits of Jesus' being dropped in. The workers are not trying to fit the Goths into a particular style of Christian community, but rather have been allowed by the Goths to join their group on their terms. In other words, the youth workers involved are not leading the group, but being part of the Goths' community. Part of their belonging to the group has involved helping the Goths in practical ways and developing good links with other relevant agencies.

This is an interesting story in that it shows failed attempts to integrate a group into what was already happening. Although the desire to involve the Goths in the existing youth group and to run an Alpha course for them was well-intentioned, ultimately something distinctive and focused around the needs of that specific cultural group was required. Strong relationships and practical compassion for the young people were key in joining in with this aspect of the *missio dei*.

There are of course downsides to this approach to work with young people. Such work might never be seen by most of the church congregation and it runs the risk of being isolated, misunderstood and demeaned. It is more time consuming than more traditional youth work, demands more resources and might involve running different groups for different young people. It is also important to balance the needs of individual groups of young people with the pitfall of simply pandering to them and encouraging a kind of consumerist approach to mission and faith.

Rick Warren explores the whole idea that when it comes to church services one size really doesn't fit all:

> It's not pandering to consumerism to offer multiple times or even styles of worship services, It's strategic and it's unselfish! It says we will do whatever it takes to reach more people for Christ. The goal is not to make it as difficult as possible but to make it as easy as possible for the unchurched to hear about Christ.[5]

This principle can and should be extended way beyond church services to ensure that work with young people is as life-changing and dynamic as possible.

Given the pressures upon resources and the shortage of volunteers to work with young people, the challenges posed by these kinds of approaches are significant and mustn't be underestimated. This makes it even more imperative to find out what God is doing with young people in a particular community, take that as a starting point and then work strategically to think through relevant and appropriate methods of reaching them. Although Christendom culture may have propagated approaches that appear relatively one-dimensional, the new spiritual and cultural context we find ourselves in demands much more creativity, innovation and diversity in terms of missional strategy.

The Homogeneous Unit Principle

The issue of whether to focus youth work on one particular group of young people or whether to aim it broadly at all young people in a community is another debate that, like questions of integration, causes much confusion and soul-searching for youth workers. The example on pages 66–7 of the work with the community of Goths is a classic illustration of what has become known as the Homogeneous Unit Principle (HUP).

The HUP is a missiological philosophy that seeks to undertake mission with a single people group at a time rather than developing a broader appeal and strategy. Originally based upon work by Donald McGavran, the hypothesis is that 'people like to become Christians without crossing racial, linguistic or class barriers'. Much has been written about this subject and it is contentious among theologians, missionaries and church-growth experts. The following table highlights the main arguments for and against the HUP.

The main arguments for and against the HUP

	Argument for HUP	Argument against HUP
Rationale	Allows focused mission with a defined group of of young people.	Allows wider engagment, which is open to all young people.
Biblical precedent	Jesus commanded us to go to people groups (Mt. 28:19). Paul sought to fit in effectively with the people groups he was working with at any point in time (1 Cor. 9:20–22).	The apostle Paul said distinctions between race, gender, wealth, etc., were no longer an issue (Gal. 3:28).
Cultural understanding	Many youth cultures and sub-cultures require culturally-appropriate responses and approaches.	Young people need to learn to be part of the wider community and integrated accordingly.
Theology of mission	Those from a particular culture know how best to work with those from the same culture.	Those outside of a particular culture might not be reached and the needy might be overlooked.
Success criteria	It works.	What happens when young people move, grow up, or change

		their loyalty to a particular group?
Diversity and inclusion	It is likely to be very inclusive for the cohort.	It lacks diversity, richness and wide experience. It is prone to exclude people who are different, thus creating a form of ecclesiastical apartheid.
Generational	Will be age-focused with appropriate resources.	Young people will not learn to appreciate different generations.
Churech	Declaring a HUP approach spurs people to mission with that cohort.	The idea of church as family will be inhibited.
Language	Colloquial approaches mean that everything is understood by those involved. Confusion is avoided and contextual commun-ication is effective.	Narrow application promotes individuality at the potential expense of the community and wider understanding.
The future	Young people grow church together into adulthood and then reach out to their peers in the wider world.	Young people don't stay in static groupings as they get older and are then unable to relate to the wider world and church.

It may be that an HUP approach will be appropriate for all or part of the mission strategy for a particular church or organization. If this is the case, it is helpful for everyone involved to be made aware of the type of work that is being undertaken with regard to the HUP. This will:

- help sharpen the focus of the mission;
- be liberating for youth workers in helping them establish and know their own boundaries;
- avoid overstretching workers who might otherwise feel under pressure to reach every young person all of the time;
- further understanding of what God is doing at a particular time;
- determine how resources are deployed;
- help establish the most relevant and appropriate ways of 'doing' church with young people.

It should be noted that the HUP debate is different from the debate about whether or not youth church or youth congregations are a good idea. The concept of youth church may in some contexts be seen as an attempt to fan the flames of the dying embers of Christendom, rather than a response to a post-Christendom position. Many expressions of youth church are still attempts to get young people into a building, to undertake corporate worship and to be a heterogeneous group, albeit one made up of young people. The HUP does not seek to do this. It focuses upon particular cultural groupings of young people rather than seeing them as a collective whole.

To illustrate this distinction, we will momentarily explore the subject of worship. While some youth churches do have a particular musical worship style, many just have a louder version of the soft rock package that is present in many adult churches. This is an heterogeneous approach. Many young people don't like this type of music and find it alienating. As one young musician said, 'I've been trying to do some more progressive worship music, but it's a struggle. Choruses have all the same chord progressions. It's not very worshipful playing the same chords in the same way all the time.'

Interestingly, many adults appear to presume that choruses played loudly are youth friendly! The HUP would seek to offer worship in the style of one particular group of young people. This worship may be musical and have a club culture feel, a grunge feel or the feel of a thousand other musical derivatives, or it may be non-musical with symbolic, liturgical, visual and/or kinaesthetic approaches.

While individuals may well have strong personal opinions on the relative merits or demerits of the HUP, it is important to acknowledge that God is not restricted and may well be at work in different ways in different communities with different groups of young people. To quote the Bishop of Oxford, Richard Harries, 'The church has put God into a box of a particular size, wrapped it in brown paper and tied the string. God is outside the box and many people have discovered this in their own spiritual yearnings and gropings.'[7] An HUP approach may be the answer to mission with one community, while a more heterogeneous approach may well be God's direction in another. Having said that, it would appear that as western Christianity becomes more marginalized, and the youth culture more fragmented, the HUP approach will have more to offer in undertaking mission with young people.

The youth worker who facilitates the work with the community of Goths in Coventry (see pages 66–7) also participates in work with young people in the local dance club culture. Having observed that the culture of even the most modern of worship services was a long way away from that of the young people who were part of the clubbing scene, a group of workers decided that it was impossible to use the existing frameworks of the church to bridge the gap. They therefore decided to begin a piece of work focused on the HUP. The vision and aim of this work is to create a community that has Christ within it, and over time to begin to grow church within this emerging community. The hope is that the work will ultimately be led by the clubbers, who will be given freedom to establish and guide all that happens.

From the youth workers' point of view, engaging with this particular group involves working until 4.30 in the morning, listening to the young people and helping them with any problems they might have. Clearly, work with groups of young people like this can only take place in the early hours of the morning and almost by default it ends up being based on the HUP. Not all youth work fits so neatly into a cultural paradigm. It is, however, possible in some situations to design youth work so that it fits into culturally distinctive patterns. It is interesting to consider the different sub-cultural cohorts of young people who might be present in a small town. A survey might reveal the following groups:

- Some might live on an ex-council housing estate.
- Some might live in pockets of executive-type housing.
- Some might be into skateboarding.
- Some might hang out at the local late-opening shop.
- One gang might be into smoking weed and dominating the local park.
- A mixed group might play football in the summer evenings.
- Some girls might like dressing up and going out at weekends.
- Some groups might be into particular kinds of music.
- One group might be defined by their race or nationality.
- Some 'anonymous' young people might spend most of their time sitting at home reading, playing music and trawling cyberspace.
- Some might play for a particular sports team, go to an activity club or special interest group.
- Some might have a disability or other special needs.
- Some might be the children of asylum seekers and/or might not have English as a first language.
- Some might be dancers, dramatists, artists or poets.
- A student group might only be around for parts of the year.

The list will differ from community to community and could be quite extensive. The key lies in recognizing that often young people fall loosely into cultural groupings that lend themselves to the HUP. Initial engagement with a group who are into skateboarding, for example, would almost by necessity demand a detached youth work approach. Doing church with them might involve staying on the street in their cultural surroundings.[8] One note of caution here. While identifying subcultural groups is very helpful for determining mission strategies, it is important not to label or box in young people in negative and destructive ways. Approaches that listen to the young people themselves and allow them to self-define help to avoid this pitfall.

Any attempt to engage all the young people listed above would require vast resources. The HUP enables workers to decide who they will work with and how this will be done. Again, a sense of listening to God and seeing where he is at work is key in approaching this process strategically.

Debates about the HUP will no doubt continue well into the post-Christendom era. It is, however, important to note that many Christians view the early church as a cohesive whole. This is in part due to the influence of Christendom thinking and interpretation. It is interesting to consider that although society in New Testament times did have some different group-ings, it was less culturally diverse and more homogenous than society today. The diversity that did exist tended to be deter-mined primarily by geographical differences. Thus the HUP model can be seen in the way the early church's approach to life, mission and values appears to have varied from town to town.

We could argue that had there been a willingness throughout church history to adopt the HUP, then Christendom would never have got such a stranglehold over the church in the west. Only a universal approach can dominate so effectively, a tailored approach being likely to engender creativity, innovation and diverse methodologies. The link between church and state has been pivotal in determining a dominant universal approach. The mere fact that Anglican churches were designed to deliver the same spiritual package in the same way, at the same time, to all the people has done much to stifle an HUP mission dynamic. It is interesting to note, however, that in recent times the Church of England has been seeking to develop and promote new ways of working, and Fresh Expressions and emerging approaches to growing church appear to embrace the very principles we are talking about.

Anecdotal evidence would seem to suggest that in current work with young people, it is the HUP form of mission that is most successful (though 'successful' is a term that is potentially ambiguous and confusing). As the church continues to lose its position of privilege and influence, it may well be that a hetero-geneous and universal approach will simply not be sustainable on any meaningful level.

Incarnational Mission

Various writers have explored what 'incarnational' might mean in terms of ministry generally and youth work in particular.[9] Some of the key issues focus around the life and ministry of Jesus. The word 'incarnation' means 'in flesh' and in Christian circles this term is most commonly used to describe God taking human form in the person of Jesus Christ (Jn. 1:14).

In a youth work context, the term 'incarnation' is often used to describe the ways in which we as youth workers can endeavour to 'be' Jesus to young people, enabling them to see Christ in us. So-called 'incarnational' approaches tend to focus on 'being' and on relationships, on seeking to 'flesh out' the gospel through identifying with people as Jesus did, being alongside them and engaging with the everyday things of their lives – their successes, sufferings, joys, sorrows, hopes, fears, struggles and celebrations. Incarnational approaches use the language and culture of the young people and often tend to embrace vulnerability, seeking to rely upon God's grace rather than on running sophisticated projects or operating big budget youth buildings and programmes.

The work with the Goths in Coventry (pages 66–7) is an excellent example of incarnational mission with young people. The workers became part of the Goths' community, shared life with them and tried to be Jesus to them, giving them time and respect, and doing this not just by proclaiming a message, but by offering practical help.

Part of the Christendom legacy has been a meeting-oriented culture in which we offer programmes, events, plans and courses. These resources have flooded the market at the very time when the decline in young people finding faith appears to have accelerated. Perhaps we have been doing something fundamentally wrong. This is a humbling possibility for those of us who have been involved in writing, developing and using some of these resources. If mission is primarily about relationships, then we need a major rethink and realignment of resources to embrace the possibilities of simply 'being' with young people.

Incarnational, relational approaches to work and mission with young people are often unglamorous. They tend not to be supported by media campaigns; they may be slow, frustrating and show little fruit for a lot of time and effort. They do, however, come with a money-back guarantee – well, almost. If we persevere, focus upon young people's needs, aspirations and interests, allow our compassion and love to grow and are led by the Holy Spirit, then we will be effective. We may not see thousands coming to faith, but experience would suggest that young people will feel valued, their potential will be enhanced, and they will see glimpses of God.

Perhaps it needs to be acknowledged that this way of thinking might simply be too great a revolution for many youth workers and churches. For some, abandoning the weekly meeting in favour of something less structured and more incarnational, however commendable, does not seem a realistic possibility. It is potentially much more demanding and requires a different set of skills.

Not only is there a call upon youth workers to be incarnational in their approach, but if we are truly to undertake mission in the post-Christendom era, then Christian young people also need to embrace this philosophy and lifestyle. We have already noted how hostile the school environment can be for Christian young people and the challenge of such an approach should not be underestimated. But there is little point in youth workers seeking to work incarnationally if they do not encourage young people to live in this way, too.

Simply equipping young people to go out into the world with an approach that seeks to drag their friends to church or to outreach events is the same old flawed strategy that has been part of 'adult-Christendom'. Rather than supporting the top-down methods that proliferated under Christendom, we need to encourage, disciple and train young people to develop positive missionary responses that engage appropriately with people and situations. Surely the aim is for them to become effective witnesses and missionaries to their peers. They are much better placed to do this than any adult.

A conversation with Lisa illustrated alarmingly what happens when an incarnational approach is not promoted. Lisa is 17 and quite up front with her peer group about her Christian faith. She is passionate about God and about trying to live out what she reads in the Bible, but at the same time she wrestles with a number of lifestyle issues and choices. She drinks a lot and takes soft drugs and by her own admission operates within a dualistic lifestyle.

Lisa was perplexed by the suggestion that she was a potential missionary to her friends and was astonished to hear that by simply being with them she could make a difference. Her understanding was that her 'job' was to make contact with her friends, engage them in conversation and then invite them to church or something similar for someone else to do the mission 'bit'.

This is Christendom at work in a particularly perturbing way in that it simply does not connect the message with an incarnate lifestyle. As Lisa said, 'If it is true about me being a missionary, then I'm crap! I thought my work was to open the door and invite my peer group to a local church.' Lisa went on to say that her beliefs did not generally affect the way she behaved.

A casual observer might jump to the conclusion that Lisa was not very motivated about God. Nothing could be further from the truth. She actually thinks that some Christian youth work compromises itself by not focusing on God all the time! She wants to serve him as best she can. She is very aware of her own failings, but no one has ever told her that *she* is the message, and the possibility of leading others into relationship with God through her own life and witness is completely foreign to her understanding.

While acknowledging the weaknesses of a programme- or activity-focused approach, we would not want to throw the proverbial baby out with the bathwater. Professional youth work acknowledges the importance of relationship-building and informal education within the context of activities and programmes and has often been more effective than church-based youth work at engaging with young people's needs. What is needed are ways of moving forward that encompass the very essence of incarnational approaches and make use of programmes and activities that actually reflect the heart of being incarnational.

In engaging with those young people who are beyond the reach of most churches, it is helpful to have an incarnational premise and as a starting point to focus purely on relationships. As these relationships develop, workers can be open to undertaking activities with the young people, and in so doing can ultimately encourage them to see themselves as incarnational missionaries. The key here is that these activities should not be focused around adult perceptions of young people's wants or needs, but should rather reflect the real wants and needs of the young people themselves. The former has the aroma of Christendom about it while the latter has more of a post-Christendom fragrance. It is focused on witness not control; journeying not settling; mission not maintenance; movement not institution.

A youth community project that has embraced such an approach is the Hot Chocolate Trust located at the Steeple Church in the centre of Dundee. Outside the church there is a grassed area that has always attracted young people. In 2001, the church became increasingly aware of these young people, but had little connection with them.

Hot Chocolate began in a small way when a youth worker undertaking training at the International Christian College in Glasgow approached the church with a view to working with young people in Dundee as a work placement for her training. The church gave the green light to this idea and the worker recruited some volunteers. They began talking to the young people, building trust with them and seeking to be hospitable. The name 'Hot Chocolate' came about as a result of this hospitality. The church opened its doors to the young people who were skating and hanging around nearby, served hot chocolate and got to know them. The idea was not a gimmick, but a clear signal that they were welcome and important.

Over time, the young people began to trust the church members, realizing that they were not just out to try to brainwash them. The church building was not well used and church members asked the young people if there was anything that they would like to use the building for. They responded by saying that they would like somewhere to practise their music. Thus the approach to the work was very much focused upon what the young people wanted; it was 'their thing'. The project grew very quickly and other initiatives were developed including arts projects, film-making, sports, workshops and summer activities.

While Hot Chocolate did not set out with a clear strategy, it did have a very clear set of values and principles, namely, enabling young people to grow, to develop, to be involved, to explore and to be supported. There was also a commitment to ensuring that the project would be open to all. The workers consider that if they had gone down the traditional, organized, adult-initiated youth programme route, the young people probably would never have got involved.

Much can be learned from the approaches taken here. Most importantly, it is the people who make the project work. There is a team of volunteers who do the majority of the work alongside paid staff. The total number of workers is small, but they are committed to the young people and the project over the long haul. The ethos is very much focused on building relationships with the young people rather than running activities and manning the building.

One of the keys to the success of the project has been its approach to working with others. It has formed many effective partnerships with both Christian and secular bodies. A nearby shopping centre, for example, has valued the project and as well as giving equipment for ongoing work, has joined with it to help young people gain work experience. Such partnerships have been invaluable in helping build the high quality work of the project and in broadening its influence. This influence has increased as those outside the church have seen church members' genuine concern for the well-being of the young people. Altogether, the impact on the local community has been massive.

The missional dynamic of the work is all about relationships. Themes are taken to provide stimulus for working with the young people and these are engaged with through various arts and media initiatives, which lead to discussions about life, God and other key issues. The project is ultimately about enabling young people to realize their full potential and this includes their spiritual potential. The project has explored the idea of the young people coming to the church as it is, but there are so many cultural barriers that there is doubt about whether they can make this journey. As we write, it is currently appraising how best to move this forward. Three young people have managed to cross the barriers and one has managed to stick it out. Some of the other young people indicate that they have a Christian faith.

This type of incarnational work with young people is exciting, stimulating and effective. It promotes values and principles that can be sustained in a post-Christendom era and establishes ways of working that embrace building positive relationships with young people.

The Message

We have already referred to the fact that young people no longer know the Christian story and have little knowledge and understanding of its theology. Paul McQuillan comments that 'young people's first language does not connect with the language of spirituality and religion'.[10] Work done by Phil Rankin has drawn similar conclusions.[11] Although in one sense this can be perceived as problematic, in another it provides a fantastic opportunity.

The problem lies in the fact that the terms used to explain the tenets of the Christian faith are not understood. The opportunity is that this lack of awareness means that the good news can be communicated in fresh and stimulating ways. Within this opportunity lies a hidden challenge: given no prior knowledge about the gospel, which element of it should we concentrate on communicating? There would seem to be a number of possibilities and perspectives:

- The evangelical/conversion element that is about a personal God and a personal faith (Rom. 10:9).
- The environmental element that seeks to respond to the fact that 'the whole creation has been groaning' (Rom. 8:18–22) and demands that we live more ethically and holistically.
- The importance of simply putting faith in God, as Noah, Abraham and the thief on the cross appear to have done. The promotion of a living faith in God without imposing any additional demands is an approach Jesus appears to take when he meets the Roman centurion (Lk. 7:1–10).
- Liberation theology, which seeks to engender freedom from oppression and deliverance for the wider community (drawing from Exodus).
- Linked to this, and echoing the voices of the Old Testament prophets, the praxis that God is a God of justice, who seeks to combat poverty, corporate abuse and feelings of powerlessness.

- The approach that seeks to reach those who have been sinned against more than they have sinned, shown in the response of Jesus to the woman caught in adultery (Jn. 8).
- Similarly, perhaps, an approach based around those who suffer – 1 Peter 4 might be helpful in this regard.
- The possibility of relationship and community with God, who offers salvation through the model of the Trinity. Note here the power of community in Acts chapters 2 and 4.

This list is not meant to confuse or to suggest that there are ways of coming to faith other than by grace. It is simply suggesting that given the fact that many young people know little about God, there are many ways of engaging with them. We need to have a clear understanding of what we believe the gospel to be if we are to communicate it effectively. It may mean that we seek to connect with various groups of young people in a whole range of ways depending on their cultural and social contexts. In terms of the *missio dei*, it may be that God wants to be different things for different young people at different times.

In the recent past, there has been a concentration upon the theology of individuals being sinners who by repenting will be forgiven and come to faith. This message has been communicated to people in a host of ways, some of which have been effective and some simply embarrassing! While no doubt doctrinally sound, this is only part of the story. Underpinning all such messages has been the assumption that people experience this guilt. Because Christendom no longer dictates society's moral 'norms', it seems as though guilt is not as prevalent as it once was. While, theologically, we are as guilty as we have ever been (Rom. 3:23), practically, many young people simply do not feel guilty. Given such a state of being, it is hard to convict people of their sin.

For example, sex is now seen as a leisure activity by some young people. They think there is nothing wrong with having multiple partners without on-going relationships. Some youth workers will have noticed that among young people there is a growing culture of differentiating between 'going out' with someone and having a 'casual relationship'. A further example is the way people continue to shop and consume like there is no tomorrow. While a minority have begun to address this issue and seek to live alternatively to the 'must have it today' and debt culture that consumes so many households, many see nothing wrong with it – and that includes many in the church. They don't feel guilty that someone in the developing world might be paying a heavy price for their consumption habits.

Although our understanding would be that it is the Holy Spirit who convicts with regard to sin (Jn. 16:8), within some churches there has often appeared to be a cultural expectation that part of the role of the Christian youth worker is to make young people feel guilty so that they may be presented with the opportunity of repenting. As Richard Harries reminds us, 'Apart from anything else, the trouble with this strategy is that the wrong people tend to feel guilty. There are some people who are beset by feelings of guilt . . . Such people need to be liberated from these irrational feelings'.[12]

Some of these feelings are not irrational, but are the result of suffering and trauma. Where guilt is felt, it is most often felt by the young people who self-harm, who abuse drugs and alcohol and have low self-esteem and they are typically victims – victims of sexual abuse or bullying. This guilt is not usually felt because of their sin, but because of the sin of others against them. Such young people need healing, not condemnation.

Confirming the absence of guilt in many young people's lives, Chris, aged 17 and a committed Christian, said:

> I give into peer pressure. I drink a lot, smoke, do drugs. General teenage stuff. I do a few other things. I do it for fun and for laughs. Because Christians don't know about it there is no one to challenge me. I need someone to challenge me, but not my parents. The pattern of my life is likely to continue as I get older and get worse. I do have cut-off points, but I don't know what they are . . . When I'm not a good witness I don't have to account. If I'm not talking about Christianity I can do what I want! It's important to compromise sometimes. I know some people who are so set apart that they can't connect to other young people. My way of connecting is going out on a Saturday night!

This may well be a strong argument for seeking to engage missionally with young people in one of the ways outlined above.

Amie summed this up most eloquently and effectively when she said:

> It's OK to concentrate on sin and guilt for Christians, but not for non-Christians. The solution is to get people into relationship with God and let him sort it all out, but it never seems to happen. The church wants people to behave in a certain way before they come to church.

Maybe it would be wiser in our mission to concentrate on learning and not teaching. There is a difference. In learning the emphasis is about the individual developing through experience and exposure to ideas, life, skills, possibilities and creativity. Teaching is about passing on information, skills and knowledge. The former is about holistic development and completeness while the latter reflects task-orientation and a focus on agenda. Sadly, many mission attempts and methods still take the teaching approach. The consequence has been that many young people have done courses and attended Bible studies but still have not integrated any learning into their wider lives. We will explore this in relation to discipleship later, but it is important to emphasize here that we need holistic, life-focused approaches to mission, not just theological pronouncements. It is highly likely that Eutychus learned more from his fall from the window, encounter with death and subsequent resurrection than he did from Paul's eloquent sermon.

God is a God of grace and while the goal may be to have Christ-like perfection, the day-to-day reality of life for most Christians is of ebbs and flows. Maybe if young people were to hear this a little more often, they wouldn't feel that the bar was so high. If we were to lose the teaching about the need to appear perfect, which is part of the Christendom culture and theology and brings with it a lack of reality, then perhaps Christian young people's self-esteem would not be so undermined. The mission statement of the Apex church network in Las Vegas has something helpful to say about this. Heading the list of things the church is passionate about is the following pronouncement: 'We all suck – we aren't good enough apart from God to do anything quite right!'[13]

It is also worth considering the question: 'What if God is already there with the young people?' Does this affect the message and the way we do things? In his work with young people, Dave Horton combines traditional Christian activity and gangster rap. Reflecting on the magic of connecting with the God who is already present among young people, he writes:

> The evening started off as usual. If anything, in fact, it was even a bit more rowdy than usual. There were nine lads sat around the living room, all of them young people we'd met through our detached youth work on the estate. They were a lively bunch, generally known by other local people for their 'difficult' behaviour. The sort of lads that people assume know 'too much about their rights and not enough about their responsibilities'.
>
> Before they arrived we had adorned the walls with contemporary images of Jesus on the cross and a quote from their favourite gangster rapper, Tupac Shakur ('God said he should send his one big odd son to lead the wild into the ways of the man'). We had also placed a big wooden cross, covered with nails, at the end of the room. We were looking for a way to make Easter real to a bunch of lads on a council estate in South Wales.
>
> We started with the traditional cup of tea, a biscuit and a couple of play fights. Next we showed Jesus' death and resurrection, courtesy of *The Miracle Maker*. A brief conversation followed about why Jesus died, punctuated by further play fighting and the odd insult about someone's mother. I wasn't feeling great about the rather reflective ideas I had been so proud of earlier while preparing for all this. Anyway, if in doubt, plough on regardless.
>
> 'OK, we're going to do something a bit different now! I'm going to hand you each a piece of paper and a pen and I want you to spend a bit of time on your own thinking about things that nag at your mind and that you can't seem to let go of. Write them down on the paper, hang them on the big old wooden cross, and walk away. Later on, when you've gone, we'll take them down and throw them away. I promise you, we won't look at them!'
>
> Oh no, what have I said? I might as well have just told them, 'Go to your rooms and think about what you've done!'
>
> As I watched the events unfold, with that familiar feeling of disappointment starting to settle over me as I felt such things as

control, success and self-esteem ebb away! I noticed that something was happening. One lad was sat in the corner writing away on his piece of paper. Slowly but surely, others started to find their own bit of space in the room with their thoughts and their pen and paper. Some lads were writing essays, some were just looking a bit confused! The atmosphere had turned and now even those that were struggling to engage with the process seemed to understand that this was a time when a bit of respect was needed for those that were busy scribbling away.

One by one the group started to come forward and hang their bits of paper off the rather gruesome looking lump of wood and nails in the corner. The evening finished with a prayer and some hot cross buns. Somehow the evening had been redeemed. Not only that, but we had involved the group in an experience, a ritual if you like, that expressed the redemption that is theirs through Jesus' death on the cross. I guess Tupac was right. God's odd son is leading the wild in the ways of the man![14]

Dave goes on to pose some key questions that are worth considering as we reflect on how we seek to convey the message: How do you enable the young people you work with to experience the reality of the gospel instead of just hearing about it? What already exists within their culture that might help you communicate with them?

In looking at this subject, we are not proposing some new heresy, nor are we appealing for a return to a message and theology of either the recent or ancient past. What we are saying is that the good news message needs to be proclaimed in context as a matter of utmost urgency. Whether we explore new angles or use traditional ones, we have to allow young people time and space to reflect upon the message rather than force an immediate response. Sally McFague argues that

> the purpose of theology is to make it possible for the gospel to be heard in our time . . . The credibility gap between thought and life, theology and personal existence, the gospel and contemporary society, is one which, given the nature of the form in which we have the Good News, never should have occurred.[15]

We concur with this analysis and trust that these gaps can be closed and young people reached for the kingdom.

Social Action

In recent times there has been a mini explosion of social action projects run by churches and Christian organizations. Young people have been at the heart of many of these initiatives. Maybe this is a move of God. Maybe it is a reaction to the fact that traditional forms of evangelism, such as street work, door knocking, seeker services, missions, outreach events, have failed to deliver the desired outcomes. As the church has wrestled with the decline associated with the end of Christendom, and a move to the margins, it appears that alternative activities have been sought. Maybe this is because we are responding in more effective ways to the challenge of engaging with young people, or perhaps the fact that people no longer come into church has finally driven the church to go to the community. Maybe it is a combination of all of these factors.

Clearly there are potential benefits to such projects. Local communities can be strengthened and improved, poverty and injustice combated and issues of powerlessness addressed. Those young people taking part in the projects can benefit significantly as they serve others and 'get their hands dirty'. The benefits to young people include:

- increased self-confidence;
- new experiences;
- meeting new people;
- exposure to challenging circumstances;
- understanding the importance of serving others;
- development of new skills;
- employment opportunities;
- the chance to make the walk match up with the talk.

> One teenager, who took part in a city-wide event organized by a major youth work agency, was so impacted by the experience that she went home and replicated the project in her own town on a local housing estate.

It is to be hoped that as the post-Christendom era gathers momentum, many more of these types of projects will be undertaken and delivered in a manner that avoids both making inaccurate assumptions and adopting the kinds of hype, branding and delivery styles that can be colonial in nature and stem from a Christendom mindset. These types of project are vital, not just because they are effective ways of engaging with young people outside the church, but because we should be doing them anyway, as acts of love and compassion for people in our communities. Indeed, if we do these kinds of projects just as a means of engaging young people so that we can evangelize them, then we will have failed. Not only are we unlikely to succeed in our objectives, but we are likely to undermine the very gospel we are seeking to communicate.[16]

The capacity of Christians to describe something as 'new' when in fact it is as old as it could be, knows no bounds. In undertaking such social action initiatives as a tool for mission in a post-Christendom era, it is important to note that they have the potential to be as thorough an embodiment of Christendom as it is possible to get. The Christendom era, which perpetuated 'coming' models of evangelism, is reflected in the approach, which does the social action bit, then tries to get the young people to a meeting or event at the end to hear the gospel, normally some sort of monologue sermon followed by an appeal to follow Jesus.

An approach more befitting culture post-Christendom would encourage workers to have an ongoing commitment to the young people in the area where they live, building community and sharing life incarnationally with them. There would not be a transient or visiting methodology, but a 'going' and 'being with' approach.

Given the value of these projects and the fact that they really can be good news for the community, they need to be carefully thought through and underpinned with a clear theology and value base. Without such preparation, the projects run the risk of merely following a trendy fad. If we are not careful, they will just be another thing for Christians to take in, consumption generously disguised as mission! As Nick Shepherd has suggested, we need to make sure both that projects like these do not end up as pieces of Christian tourism and that the young people doing them are aware of the 'tourist-missionary' challenges that surround such initiatives.[17]

Kenda Dean warns that 'compassion easily becomes Christian parachuting, a decontextualized "dropping in" to a needy situation just long enough to distribute beneficial goods that sometimes places unwanted stress on a beleaguered community'.[18] This again reminds us of the importance of long-term, strategic approaches and involvement with communities. If we just drop in for a few days, we may end up doing more harm than good. When combined with the tourist mentality, such 'parachutings' merely pander to an entertainment culture that makes those involved feel good, but runs the risk of alienating potential beneficiaries.[19]

This brings to mind a conversation we had several years ago with a youth worker who was based in a particularly challenging housing estate in an inner-city area. He was doing his best to connect with the local young people. He was educated, quite well-off and came from a very respectable family. The young people, on the other hand, struggled with education, many lived in poverty, and employment prospects were extremely limited. They said to him, 'It's all right for you. You can leave whenever you want to and go and live wherever you want. We can't. We're stuck here.'

Two years later the youth worker did leave for an affluent suburb in the Home Counties. While some might not consider two years a short period of time, it is nonetheless a very short time in the life of a community. This story unfortunately bears the hallmarks of a parachuting approach to mission. If community work focused around social action is to be attempted in short periods of time, then we would appeal to youth workers and their employers or sponsors to be aware of the limitations of this approach and the impact it will have on the community. In this community, the young people were left isolated and disappointed.

We have recently spoken with one young man who expressed deep concern that the local churches were coming to visit him and his estate to undertake a week's social action project. He lived on the estate all the time and was quite apprehensive about what was going to happen. A committed Christian, he was wrestling with the issue of predominantly affluent people jetting into his disadvantaged community. He had a very real fear that they might be seen as 'do-gooders'.

Those planning such projects need to think very carefully, with sensitivity and consideration, about the activities that will be undertaken. They should, for example, thoroughly research the area to ensure that what is planned is not already taking place in another format. Moreover, many social action projects involve doing things for free or giving things away, and though on the surface these goals are commendable, sensitivity is needed to ensure that such 'generosity' does not negatively impact the local business community. For example, a free car wash might take customers away from a business that is undertaking such work; giving away burgers might impinge upon local burger suppliers. The intentions might be good, but if local difficulties are not to be increased, lessons from around the world need to be incorporated into the planning of the projects with careful thought being given to the wider implications of the immediate 'give-aways' and marketing stunts.

If social action projects have an incarnational root, if they do not attempt to integrate young people into a distant church and if they have a clear missiological purpose, then they stand every chance of being good news in the post-Christendom era. But if they are simply another way of presenting an attractional, hit-and-run, parachuting and culturally dysfunctional form of Christianity, then they are no better than earlier failed attempts. Those involved might have a lot of fun amid the hard work of setting them up and delivering them, the projects might strengthen and equip those undertaking them, but in all likelihood they will do little for the local young people they seek to benefit. In extreme circumstances, they may even make things worse!

This point is illustrated well by John Walker, a Centre for Youth Ministry student who had cause for some honest reflections on his placement in a Christian project that was exploring the boundaries of being church with marginalized young people. He writes:

> The front end of this project is a Café – a 'coffee shop' selling tea and coffee and hot meals for homeless people. However, on Wednesday afternoons it isn't opened as a café, instead offering a time of Church for the workers and clients together. All are welcome, though asked to be sympathetic to the service.

Around ten people were there this particular Wednesday, about a half and half mix of clients and staff. The service took the form of a few guitar-led songs, the guitar played by coffee shop manager and the boss was doing a small talk, and there was time for open prayer and response.

Ten minutes in, a regular client, Sandy, appeared at the door. He was smoking, which is fine, but what he was smoking smelt suspicious. After one of the staff explained that it was 'church' this afternoon, he agreed enthusiastically and sat down. It was pretty clear Sandy was smoking weed, and was soon asked to put it out. After a couple of songs, Sandy interjected. He began by telling us that he had just taken heroin, and had been on his way home to smoke some weed and relax, when he had felt that he should come into the café. He then told us about the time he had spent in prison, and his becoming a Christian there. He talked at great length, but with enormous passion, explaining how strongly he felt that Christ had guided him into the café that afternoon, and how much he wanted to change his life.

At the end of the time, we were to sing one final song. Sandy asked if we could sing, 'Lord, I Lift Your Name on High'. The leader said, yes, fine. Sandy then asked if he could play the guitar. The leader replied, 'Can you play guitar?' Sandy confirmed, and he was given the guitar and he proceeded to play the most extraordinary guitar, intricate and alive, without the music. He led the singing, and finished with a fantastic ending, sung fantastically. As a group, we sat back and were stunned. Someone asked Sandy to keep playing, if he had anything else to play, and Sandy played his own improvised folk tunes while people cleared up.

My experience of Church is very narrow. While I've been to a number of different denominational services, the majority of my experience has been in Anglican churches (albeit reasonably forward thinking ones). I had forgotten what church was. Church is two or three gathered in Christ's name. Church is a youth group. Church is Sunday morning with organs and dust. Church is heroin addicts and alcoholics gathered to worship God. I'd forgotten that.

Working with the homeless community, the cultural differences are as extraordinary as they are obvious. When working with a diametrically different culture, there comes the idea that I must have to in some way curb my middle-class-ness, adapt myself because I fear alienating someone, that I might be in some way offensive by my very me-ness. And of course the reality is that acceptance is done by the other person. Someone coming into a café to get their only hot meal of the week accepts me, as much as I accept them. I do not ask them to wear a top hat and carry a cane before I will serve them. (I don't wear a top hat of course – it's impolite indoors). To communicate cross-culturally, first an agreement of acceptance between the two cultures must be present. Otherwise the communication is either dishonest (pretending to be other than you are), or not present.

Community

Community is important to young people. It might not, however, be the defined type of community that some adults might think of. Indeed, it might be a transient, highly mobile community or a complex network. Both secular and Christian agencies have offered young people the opportunity to become involved in a host of initiatives, programmes and schemes. What has remained throughout, as many of these ideas have come and gone, has been a simple demand from young people: something to do with their friends and somewhere to do it.

We have already referred to the fact that community among young people might take a wide variety of formats. It could be focused around gender, racial background, faith group, interest group, hobby, school, village, town or housing estate. In recent times new forms of community among young people have come to the fore with the emergence of the electronic communities based around the use of mobile phones and the internet. Some people have described these as 'virtual communities', but it could be argued that this is to do them a great injustice since for many of the people who use them, both young and old, they are not 'virtual' but extremely real. We have seen an explosion in online chat rooms such as MSN; auction sites such as e-bay; and personal profile sites such as *MySpace* and *Facebook*. Many youth workers are familiar with these communities and how they work, and many are part of them themselves.

Some youth workers are very aware of the value of engagement with these types of communities in undertaking mission with young people and facilitating mission by young people. These youth workers are as likely to spend a couple of hours in an online discussion as planning a Bible study or running a youth club. New technologies have opened up tremendous potential for undertaking discipleship, and offering encouragement and support.

Much has been made, especially by the media, of the risks to young people caused by adults entering these worlds and seeking to engage in inappropriate contact. Every precaution must of course be taken and careful thought be given to ensure the protection of all involved. But the reality is that both adult workers and young people face far greater risks when they leave the house in the morning. We should not allow fear of these risks to undermine incarnational mission with and in these communities. Good policy frameworks and accountability can help significantly in the assessment and monitoring of risk.

On a recent visit to a local centre for deaf people our eyes were caught by a series of highly effective posters that carried important messages not only for understanding and working with deaf young people, but also for reflecting on how we might help build community and work with young people in all kinds of different contexts. The six posters read as follows:

- How aware are you?
- Don't shout.
- Face the light.
- Speak clearly.
- Be patient.
- Be inclusive.

If we were looking for some pointers to how we might work with young people in their communities, this list would provide much scope for thought. In terms of mission, it is perhaps the last pointer – to be inclusive – that is worthy of particular focus. How we see young people and the church community is key.

Back in the 1950s, the following was written:

There is little difficulty in getting church members to realize that a 'closed' church club has a rightful and legitimate place in the church community. The members are 'our own young people'. But the more searching test of the true missionary spirit of many a Christian community has been the readiness or otherwise of its members to recognize that the unchurched youngsters who have crowded boisterously into its premises are part of the very constituency it was called into being to serve, and in the neglect of which the church loses its very *raison d'être*. Out of that test, not a few churches have emerged with indifferent success.[21]

Not much progress has been made with regard to mission with young people; many of these issues are still contentious today. As the influence of the church becomes more marginal and society more pluralist, the need for Christian youth workers to be inclusive becomes paramount. In the past, some workers excluded young people on a number of grounds, including behaviour, sexual orientation, age and regularity of church attendance. This is a sad reflection upon the church. This kind of exclusivity was possible in the Christendom era because of the power and influence of the church and the way in which it exercised 'ownership' over much of the territory frequented by young people. In the post-Christendom era, however, this attitude might be the exception rather than the rule as buildings are closed and facilities depleted.

A new threat to inclusivity has come about from the way a certain theology is being interpreted in some churches and organizations. In this teaching, emphasis is being laid upon the fact that individual churches and groups or networks of churches have a distinctive 'DNA', by which is meant what makes them tick, what their distinctives are and what things are, in effect, non-negotiables in terms of process, practices and beliefs. Clearly every church and organization has a DNA, just as every organization has its own culture, norms and values, and in essence this does not represent a problem. The difficulty comes when people are excluded because it is deemed that they have a different DNA from that of their church. A youth work colleague, for example, was recently invited to leave the church he was a leader at because it was declared that his DNA did not match that of his church. This could be seen as the ultimate in HUP: a church no one can join unless they are the same as everyone else! However, many of these churches would approach these issues from the point of view of conformity to a set of values, rather than missional engagement with a particular culture.

This teaching becomes particularly challenging when mission is attempted. Some interesting questions arise here. How can mission be undertaken with young people who are inevitably different in terms of DNA from the church or people doing the mission? Will they have to conform to that DNA in order to become part of the worshipping community? Does such an approach confirm the need for young people to behave before they can belong? Does it compound the dilemmas around subjects such as 'don't rock the boat', 'the message', 'incarnational mission' and many of the other issues we have been considering? If any model of DNA is to be propagated, then let it be a Jesus-centred one, not one that is based on denominational style, behaviour or the vestiges of Christendom. We would do well to remember that in seeking to do mission with young people, it should be our Christology (how we see Jesus) that determines our missiology (how we do mission), which in turn establishes our ecclesiology (how we do church). Our experience a number of years ago on a residential weekend for young people comes to mind. It aptly illustrates how we so often get this the wrong way around.

Over the weekend, the church youth workers had done a fantastic job in building a sense of community. They had managed to integrate some young people into the church youth group, and these young people, who had not previously had any experience of church, were growing in their faith. On the Sunday morning there was to be a low-key service at which the young people could tell their stories about what had happened over the weekend, and then they would all share communion together.

However, a curate from the church visited the group on the Saturday and overheard conversations about these plans. He at once declared that only those authorized by the church could give communion and forbade the leaders to hold the communion service. He then allowed no discussion, simply brushing aside all the questions posed by the youth workers running the weekend. They were reduced to tears by his belligerent and dismissive attitude and the young people were denied what had promised to be an exciting experience.

There was no attempt to find a way of reframing the service to adapt it to the missiology of the group, which was focused around participation, informality and togetherness. No consideration was given as to how Christ might have responded in this situation. Rather, the existing ecclesiology set the agenda and was used to rein in and control what was happening. The lack of grace and kindness served only to increase the youth workers' sense of frustration and hurt.

At another camp, the evenings were dedicated to helping the young people explore their faith or lack of it, and participate in prayer and worship in ways relevant to them. As the week progressed, there was a growing sense among the young people in the 11s to 14s meetings that this God who they had heard about was real, and as such they wanted to engage and meet with him.

These young people found that as they prayed things started to happen. For the first time, some of them experienced a tangible sense of God's presence and one evening when some of the other leaders wanted to come and close the meeting, they were not ready for bed but wanted to pursue God. This caused all sorts of questions to be raised in the subsequent leaders' meeting, not only about the style, content and substance of what was happening, but also around practical issues. Some consternation was expressed. Should the young people be allowed to stay up past eleven o'clock? What about the final evening when there was usually a cabaret for the whole camp? It seemed that the young people wanted to pray rather than join in the entertainment.

It was a vicar who brought the needed clarity. He reminded everyone that God often chose to move when people gathered together. For these young people, this camp was one of the only times they might ever experience this level of community and workers should not be surprised about or restrict what God was doing. The words encouraged the youth workers to give the young people space to pursue God, and in the freedom given by a wise leader God created a kind of organized chaos.

Religious protocols that are really part of an unhelpful Christendom legacy can be very destructive in their failure to support and grow community indigenously among young people.

Mission needs to be based around the life-promoting values and principles that Jesus presents and this entails seeking to work with existing communities of young people. The church bit, if it happens, can look after itself. Perhaps the young people themselves might be best placed to determine how and when church should happen.

What Will Prevail?

The analysis given above suggests some constructive ways forward for undertaking mission with young people in the post-Christendom age. As we have seen, some youth workers are already operating in the ways we have been exploring, while others have never entertained, or even heard of, these possibilities. Some will throw themselves into working in the new cultural context, while, sadly, others will continue to operate as they always have, preferring a slow and lingering demise to the risk of exchanging what they now have for the possibility of a glorious, Spirit-led, missional future.

The suggestions made above are not designed to buy us some time in the hope that revival will sweep across the western world. We need to do something now that rediscovers the paramount need for mission among young people. For some there may be difficult choices ahead. Ultimately it might come down to a very simple choice. To risk now, for the possibility of a future, or do nothing and put up closure notices in the years to come. This choice is beautifully highlighted by a parable from the Cherokee Indian tradition.

> One evening an old Cherokee told his grandson about a battle that goes on inside people. He said, 'My son, the battle is between two wolves, which live inside us all. One is Evil. It is anger, envy, jealousy, sorrow, regret, greed, lust, arrogance, self-pity, guilt, resentment, inferiority, lies, false pride, superiority, and ego. The other is Good. It is joy, peace, love, hope, serenity, humility, kindness, benevolence, empathy, generosity, truth, compassion and faith.'
>
> The grandson thought about it for a minute and then asked his grandfather, 'Which wolf wins?'
>
> The old Cherokee simply replied, 'The one you feed.'[22]

5

Resourcing Youth Work
Post-Christendom

Taking into account the current numerical decline in the western church and the increasing sense of marginalization, it is fairly safe to assume that youth work today is relatively well-resourced compared with how it might be in the future. Even now, however, many youth workers struggle with the challenges posed by unrealistic budgets, a lack of adequate and appropriate space in which to undertake work with young people and the need for suitable, willing volunteers to help with the work. We need therefore both to find creative ways of making current assets stretch further and to discover fresh approaches to resourcing youth work and making it sustainable.

The *Faith in the Community* report highlights three main concerns relating to resourcing the church in the future: 'ageing church buildings, fewer clergy, and falling congregation numbers'.[1] While this report is describing churches in rural areas, these challenges are found across different types of community and appear to be universal. With a smaller congregation donor base, it is everywhere becoming more and more difficult to meet building repair bills, salaries and pension costs, and to maintain projects and initiatives.

While some denominations are taking the necessary steps to invest for the future, others are more concerned with preserving what they have for fear of losing even that. Such a position is untenable in the long term. At the moment it seems as if there is a small window of opportunity for many denominations that still have substantial assets that could be realized and utilized for investment and resourcing purposes. Unless something changes, however, this window will not last for long.

Books, magazines and youth work conferences may well become things of the past as decline accelerates and cohorts no longer exist to support such initiatives either practically or financially. Several denominations and organizations have already found it necessary to make experienced staff redundant as traditional sources of funds have dried up and have not been replaced by new income streams. Youth officer, advisor and training posts have already been deleted from the budgets of the denominations who find themselves in the most perilous financial positions. Thus, investment in work with children and young people appears to be under threat at the very time when it is most needed.

In the UK, the Methodist Church has recently undergone severe turmoil as it has sought to reconcile these dilemmas. Staff posts were threatened and it was proposed that the church recognize its ageing congregational profile and only work with people over the age of 45. However understandable such a viewpoint might be, it brings the kiss of death for the future of the Church. As Martin Saunders, the editor of *Youthwork* magazine, asserts, 'Methodism needs a vision for youth and children's ministry that will bring the Church into the 21st Century and ensure it lasts into the 22nd Century.'[2]

The training of new workers might also be under threat. As numbers of youth workers decrease, there will inevitably be fewer workers and mentors who can train new workers. New workers themselves will therefore become increasingly rare. Organizations running gap-year schemes are already reporting a declining interest, with some schemes being cancelled or significantly amended.

Agencies that provide training for volunteers often report low take up of training opportunities, which does not bode well for the future development of workers. While demand for courses that train professional youth workers is at present quite strong, the future shortage of employment opportunities, and reduced financial resources, may well have a negative impact upon the viability of these courses. Alternatively, graduates will seek employment in secular contexts, where there tend to be higher salaries and greater long-term prospects and security. Although it is exciting to see Christians in places of influence through society as a whole, it would be sad if the churches were unable to attract youth workers with a vision to serve young people full time.

While these predictions might be sobering and a cause of concern for those who offer services and resources, comfort can be gained from the book of Acts and the early church where the privileges of significant material resources are not evident. Equally, in the many parts of the world today where the church is growing strongly both among adults and young people, Christians do not have the luxury of resources, training and facilities.

Lessons need to be learned from those organizations and institutions that have begun to respond effectively to the challenges of change. Tom Horwood, author of *The Future of the Catholic Church*, is very clear about what needs to happen, and writes, 'If faith leaders took to heart the lessons of other sectors, they would be better able to set strategies for what their communities would look like in the future.'[3] He concludes that if this were done, '[We] would inspire people to bring about a shared vision, rather than responding defensively to a crisis.'[4]

With this in mind, we will now consider in more detail how we might strategically respond to the future resourcing of youth work. When we speak of resources, we are not simply referring to money. We need to think about the role buildings might have in the future, how volunteers are engaged, motivated and sustained, how social capital is developed, how we might utilize new technologies and how new ideas might be cultivated and encouraged. Each section of this chapter ends with some questions to help us reflect on how we feel about these issues and the positive actions we might take to help us prepare for the future.

Location, Location, Location

As we have already noted, it seems that the early church did not own any buildings. A number of different locations were used, but these do not appear to have been prerequisites for mission. It seems that during the pre-Christendom era, the venues used for missional and congregational activities were chosen as need arose and according to circumstances and convenience. For example:

- Philip's conversation with the Ethiopian eunuch took place on the road in a chariot (Acts 8:26–39).
- The disciples and Paul debated with local people and officials in the synagogue (Acts 13:5,14–17; 17:17; 19:8).
- During his stay in Ephesus, Paul taught the disciples in the school of Tyrannus, thought to be a public hall used for teaching (Acts 19:9).
- In Rome, Paul hired a house or room and people visited him (Acts 28:30–31).

Unfortunately, young people today do not have access to as many facilities as adults do, and are often unwelcome in some buildings. This means that they often end up having very few places in which to meet together. Young people want things to do and places to go, but these places are in short supply. The reality is that they are increasingly discouraged from gathering together in groups because they are often perceived as a threat to local communities. This is a sad reflection upon society.

Currently, youth work takes place in a wide variety of environments, including church buildings, tatty halls, purpose-built facilities, youth clubs, mobile caravans, buses, sports centres, schools, community buildings, Outward Bound centres, skate parks, hostels and residential centres. Detached youth work is undertaken out in the community, without any need for a building or physical place in which to locate the work. However, whether or not a building is used, the need for a space for young people to be and meet together would seem to be paramount in youth work. This space might equally be the street corner, local park or parish church.

All too often expedience appears to be the deciding factor in choosing a location for youth work. If there is a room in the church building, then this is where the work nearly always takes place as it is perceived to be not only convenient but also free. Often, little consideration seems to be given to the focus and objectives of the work and the kind of space they require. Moreover, the young people themselves are often not consulted about what they would find most conducive for activities, discussion or meeting with God. Similarly, in the decision-making processes before decorating or developing space in church buildings, little consideration is given to young people's needs and preferences.

As we have already noted, our missiology tends to be determined by our ecclesiology, which then influences our Christology. This means that the way in which churches and youth workers undertake mission is often shaped by the buildings they have. This approach gives a perspective and view of Jesus that tends to be building-centred rather than lifestyle-focused. This is a big mistake and often means that drama, art, music, sport and a host of other potential approaches to work with young people are often dismissed because the buildings are not suitable.

We must start by clearly determining what it is we are trying to do with and for young people, establish what space or facility would best serve this purpose, and then, and only then, seek that space and put the vision into action. The argument that Christendom has left us with a fantastic legacy of real estate might well be true, but it may well hinder our mission. The estimated cost of maintaining church buildings in the UK is now approaching £1 billion[5] and we run the risk of putting valuable resources into maintaining the fabric of Christendom's inheritance instead of investing in people and purpose. Worse still, we may be the benefactors of facilities that are no longer fit for purpose, are alien to young people's culture and are thus huge white elephants.

A number of estate agents now specialize in selling redundant churches, while major denominations have specific departments charged with disposing of buildings that are no longer used for worship. Anyone travelling up and down the country can observe the variety of uses to which these ex-churches have been put – as residential homes, factories, museums, community buildings and places where other faith groups can gather and worship.

In one sense, this is simply yet another indication that Christendom is on the wane. It is true that new churches are being opened.[6] Some groups use older buildings, some acquire new buildings and some don't use any buildings at all. The net position, however, is one of decline and fewer venues for youth work.[7] Where churches have dwindling congregations, perhaps it would be a good idea, before they end up closing, to hand the church buildings over for work with young people. At least this would create a sense of purpose and vision, which may lead to rejuvenation. This has happened with one church in Cornwall.

It began on New Year's Day 2002, when Superintendent Minister Gareth Hill was driving along the coast in Polzeath and contemplating the future of one of the 17 churches he was responsible for. The church building was situated right on the coastline in a large area of land and had an ageing congregation of just six people. In the summer the area was swamped with tourists and surfers, many of whom were attracted by the opportunities offered by the coastline's exciting surf and water sports activities. That New Year's Day, Gareth had a vision to connect the church with the culture of the people who visited the area. Some five years later, that vision has become a reality.

A project has been established called Tubestation – a tube being the ultimate wave, which surfers crave after. With an internet café, skate area, 24/7 prayer room and plans for creative arts and extreme sports initiatives, Tubestation is the type of initiative that embraces the HUP principle, connects with culture, and is wildly creative. It is an exciting, wave-riding type of project that reflects those it is endeavouring to reach.[8] One of the directors, Henry, says that the vision is to 'help people get out of the humdrum of everyday life and experience God. The dream is to help people connect their lives with Jesus so that they are intrinsically linked through the gospel'.

While focused upon the lives of those who seek the surf, Tubestation has been supported by the existing small congregation and they are still an important part of what happens. Thus, although the project embraces the HUP principle, it goes beyond it. It is viewed as an adventure that, while embracing the best of older traditions, seeks to explore church afresh and reflect a creative God. It has utilized an old building in the type of way that effectively resources the future.

A different approach has been taken in Chellington, Bedfordshire. The Anglican church building in Chellington was erected in around 1250 and was a parish church up until the early 1970s. It was then converted into a residential centre for young people, but had to be closed in 2001 for health and safety reasons. It remained closed while it was being completely refurbished and reopened for young people in 2004.

One response to the challenges associated with trying to find a suitable space for youth work has been to have an inflatable facility! A group in a rural area of the UK has purchased an inflatable marquee that for a cost of less than £8,000 can accommodate around 100 young people. It is no big, old-fashioned, leaky white tent, but has a futuristic design that is highly appealing, adaptable and flexible. This 'building' is taken around small market towns and rural areas, is inflated in around ten minutes and serves as a mobile youth centre, worship venue, disco hall or youth drop in. When used alongside something like a mobile bus for young people, the results are particularly dynamic and versatile. If we are to embrace incarnational approaches to mission and focus on engaging with young people where they are, then this type of initiative might become more widespread.

Our own experience of trying to undertake community-based youth work without a building shows that it can be a challenging process. A few years ago we were running an open club on a Thursday evening, which initially was based in the school that most of the young people attended. This proved challenging as adult evening classes were taking place at the same time. Because of the noise levels, we were eventually asked to find alternative facilities.

We then moved to a church hall, which appeared to be ideal. However, local people complained about the young people standing outside the hall talking. One particular evening a couple of the more lively members of the group stole the keys to the hall from a team member. Although the locks were changed, we were asked to stop using this facility, too, and we were forced into a detached approach to the work until we could find and renovate our own place.

In the past, local church buildings were used as gathering points for young people, almost irrespective of whether there was any personal belief or allegiance to the congregation. The buildings were just places to go to, and the attractions were often as simple as straightforward activities and the presence of members of the opposite sex! For some, this initial contact with the church led to a journey of faith and discovery. Our experience highlights a growing reluctance to allow groups of unchurched young people through the doors. This, coupled with the closure of church buildings and the development of new housing estates, complexes and neighbourhoods where such buildings are often absent, points to a challenging future for those whose youth work models are building-dependent and focused upon a defined locality.

This is not necessarily as problematic as it might first appear. As church buildings become unavailable for youth work, other types of facility, such as the marquee described above, are being considered. This presents exciting possibilities for mission and engagement with other stakeholders in the community. An incarnational model of mission does not demand a building, but begs the question as to where young people might gather to explore their faith and worship God. Perhaps the very idea of gathering in large groups for worship is itself an over-emphasized legacy of the Christendom era. In cultures where corporate worship gatherings are forbidden, individuals have not been prevented from worshipping God and building his kingdom. Maybe when we consider forms of 'alternative worship' we could include in our thinking alternative places for worship as well as the media we will use to help the process.

The New Testament suggests that the temples of God are people, rather than buildings (see 1 Cor. 3:16; 2 Cor. 6:16). Incarnational approaches operate where people are, and in our case this means that we need to ask the fundamental question, 'Where are the young people?' One of the most obvious answers is that they are in the local schools.

We have already explored some of the challenges associated with youth work in schools. These are compounded by very intense timetable demands and the complex factors associated with behaviour, ownership and responsibility that we have highlighted. In addition, increasing pressures from pluralistic approaches to education can create fear among staff and governors when they are asked to facilitate an activity by one particular faith group. Some organizations are nevertheless exploring ways of growing church in a school context, and this is a very interesting issue to pursue.

In some countries, the picture is even more complex than in the UK. In the United States, for example, the complete separation of church and state means that opportunities for Christians to work in schools are severely limited, and overtly Christian work is often restricted, if not impossible. There has been a great deal of debate about 'prayer in schools', the outcome of which has been that such prayers have been ruled unconstitutional by the US courts. In France, the law has gone further, now banning the wearing of religious symbols by pupils. In countries where Christians are not allowed to undertake schools work or to use their facilities, finding appropriate space for work with young people is a further significant challenge.

The Christendom legacy has left us a large collection of buildings in various states of repair and disrepair, and these cannot be ignored. Yet maintenance costs are prohibitive. Perhaps this, and all the other factors outlined above, point to the fact that we need to concentrate on developing models of work that focus wholly on people as the primary resource. In one sense, we should always have done this. The end of the Christendom era, however, provides opportunity to appraise our methodologies and reassess what it is we are trying to do and with whom.

For reflection and action

- In what ways would it be helpful for you to change the locations you use for your youth work? How would it affect your work positively or negatively if you made it more mobile or detached?
- If you are currently involved in a church, what do you think would be the reaction of the leadership and/or congregation to selling the building and using the money to build or buy a purpose-built youth facility that could also be adapted for worship use on Sundays?
- Take a moment to think forward 15 years. Imagine that you are still working with young people in the place where you are now. What do you think will be happening? What will be different? How do your answers make you feel?

- Consider obtaining a map of the area you work in and copy it so it is large enough to cover a table. Then think about where the young people of the area spend their time and mark these places on the map. Alternatively, do some survey work by driving or walking around the area to find out where local young people hang out. What could you do with the results of your findings?
- Why not gather a small group of people together and walk around the area where you work with young people. Look at the facilities, amenities and buildings that the area has to offer. Is God drawing your attention to any particular building and/or awakening a new vision for your work?

Imagine All the People . . .

It is almost a cliché to say that youth work is about relationships and church is about people. Although this is true in theory, clear theologically and necessary for our spiritual development, actual youth work and church practice can tend to tell a different story, as we have already highlighted. One area denominational worker reports that of the 400 or so churches that he seeks to work with, only around 40 do any significant work with young people aged 13 and over, and volunteers to undertake such work are in short supply. Clearly something is amiss. Future resourcing of youth work needs to be focused clearly and primarily upon young people and those who work with them, not upon maintaining institutions, unhelpful traditions and archaic buildings.

At this point, it might be helpful to recap and consider how things may be for those seeking to work with young people in the post-Christendom era.

- Resources may be scarce.
- Young people may well be increasingly absent from our churches.
- Some churches may be very successful in their work with young people, but the majority may not work with young people at all.

- The work that does take place may well be in the context of more formal and legislative demands that may hinder recruitment of volunteers.
- Those who do work with young people may be more overworked.
- Delivering work with young people, particularly when done in partnership with secular bodies, may put a further strain on resources as monitoring, evaluative, administrative and cost-effective assessment regimes are required.
- There may be significant opportunities to undertake mission with young people, with lots of experimental approaches.

Volunteers are already the life blood of many organizations and churches but if resources are going to be in short supply, then it is likely that there will be more reliance on volunteers than on paid workers. If youth work is to be sustained into the future, then investment needs to be put into recruiting youth workers. Both volunteers and employed staff need to be better recruited, better managed, better rewarded, better encouraged and better trained! These processes must be underpinned with good governance structures and principles of empowerment and participation. Above all, there should be a commitment to seeing those who work with young people as among the most valuable of all the church's resources.

Sadly, stories of volunteers feeling disillusioned and let down are all too common. One conversation with a denominational youth officer reflected his frustration that churches he was working with did not even view people as volunteers. It was simply taken for granted that church members would give service as an expression of their faith. Resourcing, training or supporting did not even enter the equation. This view is by no means uncommon and is reflected in the disillusionment and weariness of many volunteers. Some feel they were railroaded or guilt-tripped into helping out in the first place. Some volunteer on a short-term basis and find themselves locked into years of service. Others have bad experiences and get hurt because of young people's attitudes and behaviour, lack of support and encouragement and the sheer challenge of trying to balance the many demands of a busy life.

Churches and organizations that manage to recruit, train and support volunteers effectively appear to have a number of factors in common. The following suggestions are for those wishing to develop a strategy for recruiting, valuing and retaining volunteer workers:

- Have a clear vision that potential volunteers can relate to and 'own'.
- Adopt a procedure for new applicants, including an interview process, a check with the Criminal Records Bureau and an induction course.
- Train volunteers and get them in post as soon as possible to maximize enthusiasm.
- Recognize the service that volunteers have given. Consider celebratory meals and events, certificates, thank-you cards, emails and letters of appreciation and team away-days.
- Repeatedly encourage the volunteers.
- Communicate regularly – by phone, email and newsletters.
- Provide clear guidance, expectations and supervision – agree levels of commitment, length of service and extent of involvement.
- Value volunteers as individuals, and encourage them to serve in ways that reflect and use their personalities and skills.
- Set up volunteer schemes specifically for young people.
- Involve volunteers in decision making – seek their counsel and advice.
- Always be on the lookout to recruit new volunteers.
- Focus on the needs of the volunteer as well as the needs of the church, organization or young people.[9]

All too often people have a very particular image in their mind when it comes to youth workers. It is often easy to think of them as energetic, in their twenties or thirties, wearing trendy clothes and having a full working knowledge of the latest gadgets and popular music. This does a great disservice to the many who don't fit this stereotype, and runs the risk of actually preventing others volunteering. In the post-Christendom era we cannot afford to discourage anyone, of whatever age, background or skills, who has something to offer young people.[10]

In one of the English National Parks there lies a small, tranquil village that is a favourite watering hole of the tourists who visit the area in their thousands. Amid the rolling green hills and idyllic country cottages live a number of young people who present some very serious behavioural challenges. The village has given up on them and they have gained a reputation as the worst young people in the whole area. The only people who work with them are a retired couple and a middle-aged woman, supported by an octogenarian! Through their care, compassion and concern for these young people they are building relationships with them and are seeking to help them. Having tried a number of approaches, they are now looking to restore a small, old stone building to open a facility that the young people can use as a drop-in and call their own. The building only measures 20 feet by 10 feet but it is full of potential and is backed by vision and commitment. It has now been restored and opened. People such as these are the ones who build the kingdom.

It was Martin Luther King who said that to serve others, you 'only need a heart full of grace and a soul generated by love'. When we consider how we might resource work with young people post-Christendom, it is perhaps these qualities that most need to be propagated.

For reflection and action

- When you look back at your youth work experiences, either as a volunteer or employee, how do you feel?
- What lessons do you think you have learned and how could you pass these on to others in the future?
- Spend a few minutes thinking about all the positives and negatives of working with young people either as a volunteer or as an employee – list your thoughts. Reflect upon your list and pray about what you have written. What else could you do with these lists?
- Does the project you work on or the church you are involved with have a procedure for recruiting and supervising volunteers? If not, why not set up a process that adds value to volunteering and fosters personal growth, training and development?
- Why not undertake to facilitate at least one event in the coming year that gathers together all those involved in work with

young people in your church, organization and/or area and celebrates the work you do?

- Additionally, why not organize an event, activity or promotion that deliberately seeks to get more people involved in working with young people?

Social Capital

Robert Putnam is credited with developing the idea of 'social capital'. This term has been defined as 'the glue that holds society together', a description, interestingly, that was initially used in relation to the church. That the church is no longer seen as being this 'glue' is perhaps further evidence of a decline in Christendom.

Putnam has said that the main activities of western life in the twenty-first century – sleeping, working and shopping – can be summarized in a triangular model.

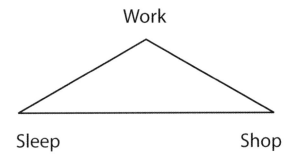

High social capital

He explains that when the majority of people work in the community in which they also sleep and shop, then the social capital in that community will be high – that is, interaction between people will be frequent, contacts will be close and regular and this will engender greater ownership, loyalty and association within the community. This is represented by the small triangle. However, when people work in a different community from the one where they sleep and when they shop in yet another community, then this lessens social capital. This is represented by the more widely-spaced triangle.

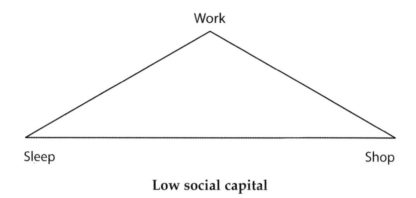

Low social capital

The theory is that the greater the geographical distance between these core activities in the lives of individuals, then the less likely it will be that strong and cohesive communities will grow and develop. We can illustrate this with the example of a family from a small town. One partner sleeps in the town, but works 25 miles away in the city. Both partners shop at the supermarket 5 miles down the road and never visit the local shop and post office. Their lives are based upon purpose networks as opposed to geographical communities.

If we then put into the equation the fact that the family go to church in another nearby town, the picture becomes even more complex. They now live their lives in four distinct networks, none of which are in the same geographical location. Apart from sleeping and watching TV, the family do virtually nothing in their locality. In terms of seeking to be incarnational where they live, they have become dysfunctional, largely because they have no effective relationships there. This erodes social capital and threatens the heartbeat of local communities, leaving them open to the accusation of being soulless. It also begs the question as to where this family might undertake mission.

If the young people from such families play sport in another area or town, travel to be part of special activity groups and have extended family members who live many miles away, then the situation will be even worse. In such circumstances it is not hard to see how young people can feel alienated, wrestle with their sense of roots and identity and begin to wonder where they belong.

Such scenarios are now common, and represent a huge cultural shift from the past, when most people carried out their lives in small, tight-knit communities. This is evidenced by recent research, which indicates that most people don't know their neighbours very well. According to the survey, a third of the people questioned have never spoken to their neighbours and 55 per cent don't know their neighbours' names.[12] These are clear indications that social capital is in severe decline.

If we now apply this model to young people, replacing 'work' with 'school' and introducing 'church' as a fourth key component, we have the following diagram.

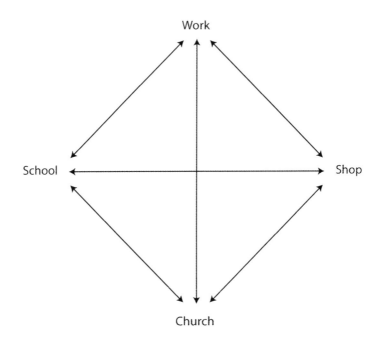

Social capital among young people

Some young people will sleep, shop, go to school and access church within a very limited geographical area, while for others this region might encompass an area of many miles. This has huge implications for how youth work is undertaken and resourced, particularly when there is considerable variation within one small group. A number of key questions emerge here.

- Where should mission be focused or undertaken? In the locality of the church or where young people sleep, go to school or shop?
- How can youth work best be resourced and provided for in areas where there is a wide geographical spread of the sleep/school/church/shop components?
- Will youth work in the future take place in more mobile ways, in terms of transient communities, rather than maintaining fixed building-centred approaches?
- Are young people's identities associated more with their networks than with a geographical locality?
- Given the near hysteria associated with child-protection issues, how might youth work be effectively and safely undertaken where transport is a problem, for example, where a group is geographically widely spread and youth workers wish to transport young people in vehicles?
- Is it realistic to sustain youth work in locations where there are only small numbers of young people or should a 'Tescoization' process be encouraged?
- Can youth work be done in one location and be supported by technology across a number of villages or towns?

These are complex and demanding questions, which will require careful consideration both now and in the future. Failure to grapple with these issues will waste precious resources and valuable time. Decisions need to be based upon the needs of young people, and buildings used only if helpful for the young people themselves and the processes of engaging with them.

The New Testament is full of stories about the use of homes as centres of missional activity, discipleship and community.[13] This approach may be significant for the future of youth work. Youth work practice must, of course, insist on the highest standards. However, recent knee-jerk reactions to child protection issues associated with working in houses have adversely affected many initiatives.

The famous Liverpool football manger, Bill Shankly, once said that he wanted Liverpool's football stadium – Anfield – to be a 'bastion of invincibility'. He nearly achieved this during his great days in the 1970s when his team dominated both domestic and European competitions. Today people seem to have adopted the same approach to their houses! Crime and the fear of crime threaten to deprive us of freedoms we took for granted in the past. Many homes have become fortress-like with fences, hedges and burglar alarms, which make them uninviting. All this contributes to   people not talking to one another, let alone loving one another. The consequence is that another valuable resource for youth work is potentially lost. This approach would seem to be very much at odds with developing social capital, and fostering shalom in our communities. Working in homes can be done safely and securely and policies need to be developed to ensure that this can happen so that homes may continue to be opened up to young people.

For reflection and action

- How do you feel about the social changes that have taken place in western society over the last few decades? In what ways have these changes impacted you and the young people you serve?
- How do you think society will continue to change in the post-Christendom era? What actions do you think you will need to take to respond to these changes?
- Would you be willing to use your home more for work with young people? If so, what steps would you need to take to ensure that this work is done safely and appropriately?
- What could you and your church or organization do to help restore the 'glue that holds society together'?
- Why not facilitate an event, exhibition, programme or activity that promotes the role of young people in the community? Young people could be asked to plan the event, liaise with the media, write stories, take photographs, prepare artwork and craft something that is imaginative and impacting.

Heroes of the Faith

> To journey without being changed is to be a nomad. To change without journeying is to be a chameleon. To journey and be transformed is to be a pilgrim.
>
> Mark Nepo

In chapter 10 of Matthew's Gospel, we see Jesus sending out his disciples into the surrounding area. They are given precise instructions and simply sent on their way. Luke chapter 10 shows seventy-two others also being sent out. Similarly, in the book of Acts we see Peter and Paul setting off on their missionary journeys. Perhaps we are moving to a season where the kingdom will be resourced by travelling youth work pilgrims who, guided by the Spirit, wander from place to place. Maybe we need a new sense of pilgrimage that embraces these sentiments. Leonard Sweet has talked of 'postmodern pilgrims' but perhaps this sentiment needs to be reframed towards resourcing post-Christendom pilgrims.[14]

Dave Wiles and Tim Evans have undertaken pilgrimages over the last couple of years. With no money in their pockets, they have set off walking, and simply talked to as many young people as they could on the journey. These pilgrimages have attracted media interest and established that young people value adults engaging with them. Stories of hope and pain have been told by the young people with a very clear sense that they have few people who will listen to them and give them time and space.

Such an approach to resourcing future work with young people is probably not for everyone, but it reconnects with the monastic orders and traditions of movements such as the Celts, Jesuits, Franciscans and Dominicans. It follows the church-building principles of Wesley and Whitefield in the eighteenth century, and a way of working adopted by missionaries throughout the ages. By so doing it reaches people who would otherwise never be engaged, literally taking good news to the highways and byways. In the future, this approach may be the only way of connecting with some young people who would otherwise not come into contact with any Christians.

Barbara and Tom Butler, in describing the spiritual activities and practices of people around the world, have helpfully framed their thoughts and stories around the following themes:

- sacred journeys
- sacred mountain
- sacred land
- sacred suffering
- sacred silence
- sacred worship
- sacred community
- sacred work
- sacred 'bovines'.[15]

By so doing, they have taken the ordinary everyday things of life and painted pictures of how people undertake the spiritual in these contexts. Perhaps in days to come, the only resources youth workers will have will be the everyday things around them and they might use these to help young people connect spiritually. In one sense, we would hope that this approach is already being followed by youth workers. It is an approach that very much resembles the ministry of Jesus. Sharing food together, telling stories, learning from one another and being on pilgrimage can all contribute to a dynamic and sustainable approach to mission with young people. Such approaches might also be combined with technology to develop ways of working that encompass cyber prophets and bloggers, technological monks and nuns, online monasticism and virtual electronic portals of refreshment and reflection.

Many heroes of the faith from Bible times and from church history had journeying as a core component of what they were about. No doubt much of this was a sign of the times that they lived in. Nevertheless, many of the elements of their ministries are transferable to post-Christendom cultures. We can all be led by the Spirit, stay and live in houses and communities where we receive a welcome, take an organic approach to ministry that doesn't rely on formulaic and prescriptive regimes and seek out God in the everyday. We will probably feel like exiles in a foreign land, but that is one of the calls of mission.

Such an approach might seem a long way away from current practice, and for many youth workers it would be a major departure. In the 1990s, we had the privilege of working with a number of communities in Spain that followed such a pattern of work. What started as an expression of compassion by a couple of people became a community of hundreds, then a movement that spread across Spain and then the world. The movement sought to take Jesus to people who would not otherwise have heard of him, and worked with prostitutes, drug addicts, alcoholics, the destitute, broken and marginalized. It relied upon a network of hubs and bases, which 'pilgrims' travelled between until the hubs could sustain themselves. Once established, these hubs would then reach out in similar ways to other communities.[16]

This model presented many practical and logistical challenges, but it worked and still works to this day. It encompasses in the fullest way possible the five-fold ministry approach endorsed in Ephesians 4:11 and resembles the pattern of mission that Paul undertook in the book of Acts. It might be worth revisiting such biblical patterns as a way of exploring and resourcing youth work post-Christendom.

As a final word on this aspect of resourcing, we would encourage you to empty your mind of images of monks in sackcloth, hermits with long beards and eccentric prophetic figures doing strange acts in public! While there is nothing wrong with such images and practices, the pilgrims of today generally look nothing like this. Today's pilgrims need to connect and engage with contemporary culture. Every year at the Glastonbury music festival, groups of Christians undertake these kinds of pilgrimages, setting up tents and marquees and engaging with visitors to the site. They provide sanctuary, a listening ear, drinks of water, sleeping accommodation for those who need it and a safe place for those suffering from the after-effects of drink and drugs. This is a type of pilgrimage that ends up establishing temporary community and connects the Christian faith with the culture of the day.

For reflection and action

- How would you have felt if you were one of the disciples Jesus sent out into a hostile world with no money and no plan of where to go? In what ways does this scenario connect with the work you are doing now?

- What does the phrase 'organic ministry' mean to you? If your ministry with young people were to become more organic, what might it look like?
- What do you think about what Barbara and Tom Butler say? What things of the everyday, ordinary landscape and world you live in can be used to connect with young people's spirituality and faith journeys to help resource work with them in the future?
- Why not undertake a pilgrimage yourself, with others or with the young people you work with? Plan something that is culturally appropriate or challenging for your context.
- To what extent does the ministry you undertake with young people encompass the five-fold components of apostle, prophet, evangelist, prophet and teacher? If there are some gaps in these components, what can you do to bring these elements into your work in the future?

Technology

We have already referred to some of the ways in which technology has impacted the world young people live in, and we have talked about how it might be used to facilitate mission with young people. Given these impacts, it would be foolhardy not to consider how technology could be used more effectively to resource work with young people post-Christendom.

Many misconceptions appear to surround the use of technology in youth work. Some see computers as the miraculous solution to virtually every problem, while others feel strongly that the use of technology depersonalizes relationships and should be discouraged. Neither of these polarized viewpoints is particularly helpful. The key issue to address is how technology can be used to make our youth work more effective in this new era. The term 'reengineering' is helpful as we consider how youth work and church need to be changed to adapt to the challenges of a post-Christendom culture.[17]

It is likely that within the next decade or so access to the internet will be universal in the western world. Currently, 53 per cent of individuals in western Europe have access, while in the United States, 84 million adults have high-speed internet access at home. South Korea is the world's current top broadband user with nearly 90 per cent of its households online. Eastern Europe, China, Brazil and Russia are showing access rate growth of up to 30 per cent per annum. The developing world is showing some growth in access rates, but the rates are slow compared to others. It is hoped that mobile phone access will help speed up connection rates in these areas.

Between them, MSN Hotmail and Yahoo! Mail have over 110,000,000 unique users registered with them.[18] The amount of music, and number of films and books downloaded grows each year. Facebook, Twitter, Habbo, Secondlife and YouTube may be modern fads, but they have changed the way many people respond to life, relationships and the world.[19] Education is being increasingly facilitated by e-learning. These developments point to unique tools, which can help us work with young people in new and creative ways that would have been unimaginable a few years ago.

As we seek to grasp the impact of technology, it is helpful to be aware that:

- more emails are now sent in the west than posted mail;
- 'word-of-mouth' is no longer spoken – it is texted and emailed;
- 4.5 billion (and rising) SMS texts are sent each month in the UK;
- 2.7 trillion emails a year are sent in the USA;
- many people can now watch any TV programme they want to whenever they want to;
- the music industry has undergone a huge transformation as a result of downloading;
- new industries now exist – gaming, online gambling, social networking;
- abbreviations now dominate our language – DVD, MP3, JPEG, i-Pod, PDA;
- you can vote, find a partner, pay your bills, pursue your hobby, purchase just about everything, study, get a job, process your family photos, work, play games and watch your favourite films without ever leaving the house!

In thinking about youth work in the future, it is important to remember that it is young people who are often the most technologically literate and it is at them that many of these products are targeted. The technology that was new yesteryear rapidly becomes commonplace and is considered essential to life itself. Mobile phones are a good example.

Anecdotal evidence suggests that some youth workers are resistant to the use of technology to support their work, fearing that it will somehow impact negatively upon what they are seeking to do. The media have tended to be preoccupied with the problems associated with new technologies, highlighting the dangers of pornography, grooming, happy-slapping and on-line bullying, as well as websites that promote suicide and eating disorders. In the light of all this, a reluctance to embrace new technologies is understandable. However, we also need to identify the positives that technology can offer both adults and young people. These include:

- increased speed and quality of information flow;
- unprecedented access to information, services and relationships;
- improvement of social connectedness and the development of new social networks;
- creation of new communities;
- new opportunities to develop and promote learning;
- a voice given to young people who might otherwise not have a chance to speak;
- some young people enabled to be more open and honest about themselves and their situations;
- engagement with young people who might otherwise be hard to reach;
- new opportunities to be, see, sense and do;
- people treated equally;
- increased sense of being included;
- facilitation of direct feedback from young people about what they want, need and think;
- opportunities for creativity and innovation;
- tailoring of information and services to the individual needs of young people;

- creation of mechanisms for democratic processes;
- opportunities to handle sensitive enquiries and requests discreetly.

In some contexts, these advantages can go a long way towards compensating for some of the youth work resources and opportunities that might be lacking. For example, in remote and rural areas, online communities have become lifelines for many, and enable workers to keep in contact with young people. In addition, we have found that when workers use the same communication tools as the young people they seek to work with, then constructive dialogue is more likely to take place. For example, if a group of young people uses one particular chat room, then it would be prudent for the worker to use the same portal. Over time, the portals used by the young people will change (technological brand loyalty not being a trait of an up-and-coming, technologically-literate generation) and workers will have to adapt accordingly.

Research undertaken in Canada has revealed that young people find these forms of communication 'socially rewarding'.[20] As such, they are part of everyday life. Older generations used to chat over the garden fence, then people phoned each other for a natter. Now young people text and use social networking for the same purpose.

When describing the role that texting plays in his youth work, one youth worker said that there are two key young people in the group, whose friends text them beforehand to find out if they are planning to attend. If either of the two young people is not planning to come, their respective friends will also stay away. Before mobile phones, this would not have been an issue.

Experts recommend that those intending to use technology draw up a plan to ensure that what is implemented is the best possible response to their needs. We would recommend that youth workers begin to take this approach, and see that the development of technology is as important as the development of other aspects of youth work, so that future work can be resourced in the most effective, sustainable and affordable way.

A typical technology plan would consider:

- what the vision is for the work with young people;
- how technology will help achieve this vision;
- what the technological requirements are;
- what funding will be available;
- how the technology is to be purchased;
- how the people are to be trained to use it;
- how to evaluate its success and ensure continued learning.

It is tempting to hand over responsibility for technology to the technical people. This can be a mistake. They can advise and inform, but ultimately everyone involved in the work with young people needs to own what is proposed and ensure that the use of technology helps achieve the youth work vision rather than take over from it. This means involving young people, creative people, youth workers and those who control the budget. There have been too many incidents of technological equipment being purchased only for it to sit in a corner because few know how to use it or because it is discovered to be not fit for purpose and of no help in fulfilling the overall vision.

For reflection and action

- What do you feel about the growth in the use of technology that has taken place over the last ten years? How do you think this has impacted the young people you know and work with?
- If technology continues to change and develop in the next ten years, what sorts of things do you think will be taking place?
- What new skills and/or equipment do you think you will need to acquire in the future?
- If you haven't got one, why not draw up a 'technology plan' for your youth work and act upon its conclusions and recommendations?
- Why not invite the young people you work with to set up a MySpace web site or Facebook group to describe and discuss the work the church or organization does with them? Resist any inclination to edit it but reflect upon what it says and how it develops.

New Ideas

In any institution – and this includes the church – problems begin when new ideas are not developed and incorporated into its life and work. Many youth workers are renowned for their inspirational thinking and creativity. Many, however, still do not invest in such processes and the churches or organizations they work for and serve are often resistant to new suggestions. Many youth workers have become disillusioned, and have even given up working with young people, because of internal opposition to doing things differently. George Pitcher, curate at St Bride's, London, has commented, 'The church isn't good at change. There are now glaciers moving with greater pace than that with which our church is embracing social change.'[21] This is a sad reflection on our levels of responsiveness.

It was Oscar Wilde who declared, 'An idea that is not dangerous is unworthy of being called an idea at all.' The message of Jesus was not a safe one. It was dangerous. It bred revolution, turned the social world of the day upside down, challenged establishment protocols and created martyrs. The implicit danger in the good news needs to be rediscovered. Youth workers are ideally placed to begin such exploring in the uncharted waters of ideas brought by young people's minds and energies.

In France at the end of the nineteenth century, there was widespread discontent among Parisian painters, writers and poets. They were frustrated, disillusioned and disheartened by the bourgeois aristocracy of the time. The artists were so at odds with society and culture that they set up a counter-culture movement that was to transform not only the world of art, but French and European society as a whole. They became known as the Bohemians.

Giving rise to philosophers, writers, and artists such Toulouse-Lautrec, Picasso and Matisse and the composer Puccini, the Bohemian movement challenged the thinking of the day and released creativity and inspiration in innovative and enterprising ways. Many of its ideas were discussed and debated in the cafés of Paris, which became much more than places to drink coffee. They were places for exchanging ideas, dreaming dreams, addressing anxiety and creating a new cultural movement, which was to impact the rest of history.[22] Some commentators draw striking comparisons between the rise of postmodernism and the attitudes and work of the Bohemians.[23]

The Bohemian movement emerged because of frustration with the status quo, the staleness of institutional bodies, the negative influence of a powerful and privileged minority over the wider society, a lack of creativity and free expression, the desire to control any radical thought and the absence of genuine communities. The parallels with the challenges that the Christendom mindset brings to the table cannot be overlooked.

The Bohemians encompassed eccentricity; they embraced the unusual and prospered in the informal. At the same time, they brought in dynamism, colour, an underworld of bedazzlement, and ideals of truth, beauty and freedom. It is true that the Bohemians lived lives that were morally at odds with mainstream Christian teaching, indulging as they did in excessive drinking, extra-marital sex, law-breaking and an abandonment of personal hygiene protocols. Conservative and Republican critics would no doubt go further and have a field day disparaging much of what Bohemianism was about. It would be unfortunate, however, if these negative thoughts and 'values' overrode any investigation into the spirit behind the Bohemian movement and the insights it can offer us today. In terms of resourcing the post-Christendom church and work with young people, the movement has much to say and many ideas worthy of consideration and rediscovery.

The Bohemians were characterized by:

- creativity;
- propagation of new ideas;
- the fusing of multiple concepts with traditional perspectives;
- expressions of community;
- promotion of subversive approaches;
- connecting with contemporary culture;
- experimentation with new ideals;
- being anti-establishment;
- abandonment of 'sentimental considerations';[24]
- a certain positive dysfunctionality;
- being confrontational;

- a tendency to be impious;
- promotion of an element of discord with society;
- withdrawal from conventionality.

Such characteristics would serve work with young people well if they could be incorporated into post-Christendom thinking. A similar resourcing of ideas is necessary if the malaise of Christendom is to be challenged and a new era begun. The Bohemians chose to live in marginal ways and created communities of practice that embraced poverty and artistry. This, too, may help our future thinking about working with young people. If the post-Christendom church finds itself short of resources, then such innovative approaches and sharing of ideas will need to be incorporated into its strategies.

There is a strong case for arguing that the Bohemian spirit needs to be prophetically released again in work with young people. Many of the Bohemian characteristics listed above could be used to sum up the traits of the Old Testament prophets and the methodologies that God inspired them to use. They are also resonant of the New Testament disciples and apostles. The tendency of Christendom to promote conformity has been to the detriment of such thinking and approaches.

In some of their recent initiatives, Frontier Youth Trust have sought to capture and build upon some aspects of Bohemian thinking. They have developed consultation processes that focus around gathering people together, encouraging conversations and seeking to create spaces where creative, innovative and unconventional thinking can be drawn out and explored. Priority has been given to resourcing methodologies that overcome fear, develop diversity, value participation and encourage broader influence within churches, Christian organizations and government policy.

This has involved undertaking a series of gatherings called 'Coffee Shop Theology' where youth workers have come together with no fixed agenda to explore issues that are important to them. Such approaches have sought to combat the top-down and often dictatorial approaches to learning that have dominated Christendom and replace them with the Bohemian traits of free speech, creative thinking and mutual inspiration. Youth workers have responded very positively to these ideas and now run café groups under their own initiative in various locations.

If the stranglehold of Christendom over the western church is to be challenged, then an approach akin to that adopted by the Bohemian pioneers of yesteryear may serve the purpose well. Young poets, prophets, writers, artists and mould-breakers need to be empowered, trusted and released.

For reflection and action

- When you think about a Bohemian approach, how do you respond? What risks might be involved? What possibilities might these approaches allow?
- Think about how your thinking has been shaped and influenced during your life. Do you need to take some time out, do something different, explore new avenues in order to expand the way you think and do things? What might you do to assist this process?
- Think about some of the past dreams that you have had. If they need resurrecting, then get them out, dust them off and set about doing something towards achieving those dreams.
- How about organizing an activity or gathering that seeks to 'release a Bohemian spirit' in those who attend. It could have a theme, a dress code, take place in a stimulating environment and/or be something that is outside of normal comfort zones. Write up the things that are discussed during this activity and any conclusions reached.

6

Church Youth Work
Post-Christendom

In this chapter, we aim to draw together the ideas we have raised through the preceding chapters. We have looked at the impact of Christendom on youth work and young people, considered current culture and some of its implications for young people, identified some possible approaches to mission with young people post-Christendom and highlighted some of the challenges posed in terms of resourcing work with young people.

Throughout these chapters, the church has been present on the edge of our analysis – sometimes provoking questions, at other times simply present as part of a broader picture. As we draw the strands of our thinking together, we now move on to focus more specifically on issues facing churches in terms of their work with young people in this post-Christendom era. What might church youth work look like? How do churches respond to the challenges that face them in their work with young people? How might they engage effectively with the issues and questions we have discussed and find a way of enabling their youth work not only to survive but to thrive in this emerging culture?

We are aware as we write that even to speak of 'church' raises problems since the word evokes a wide range of responses. For some, the term is loaded with emotional resonance, rousing powerful feelings of a positive or negative nature. Some will be eager to protect and preserve inherited images or models; others, weary of existing structures, will be seeking new ways of being and working that feel more connected to life in the twenty-first century. Our intention is not to engage in a wholesale critique of current church practice and trends, but rather to consider specific issues relating to work with young people.

We first want to highlight the key issue of process, which provides a helpful framework for looking at youth work in a church context. After considering one example of an approach to growing church with young people that has a strong missional edge, we will move on to look at broader principles relating to church youth work post-Christendom, highlighting examples of effective work and drawing out learning principles for those engaged or seeking to engage in this important work.

Process or Product?

The dictionary defines process as 'a series of changes by which something develops (the process of growth) and a method of doing something in which there are a number of steps'. Product is defined as 'something produced by nature or by people'.[1]

Emphasizing product can be viewed as a Christendom legacy. Typically, in work with young people, this might mean a focus on conversion, baptism (in water and/or the Holy Spirit), attendance at a Sunday worship service, production of a youth service, participation in a course, programme or residential experience or undertaking a role in church activities. When given time and space to reflect, many youth workers express concern that they are put under pressure to ensure that these 'products' are delivered in and through their work.

Often the process aspects of youth work – spending time with young people, coming alongside them, helping them in the everyday challenges of Christian living – are hidden from the congregation as a whole, much of what is valuable therefore being unseen. Most youth workers appear to value and enjoy the process more than the product. If youth work is to be effective, process needs to be similarly recognized and valued by the church.

The following table highlights the differences between process and product in youth work contexts. In the table the two are polarized but it is important to recognize that we are dealing with two ends of a continuum and that there are a range of approaches between the two extremes.

Approaches to youth work

Process-oriented youth work	Product-oriented youth work
Organic development is encouraged and outcomes might be wide-ranging and unexpected.	Plans are fixed and outcomes are fixed. Success is gauged against these fixed outcomes.
Relationships are valued and affirmed as important for their own sake.	Relationships tend to be built around tasks with a strong functional emphasis.
Exploratory inquisition, 'wandering' and journeying are encouraged.	Journeys are 'mapped out' with destinations and expectations fixed.
Work tends to be about young people's development and empowerment.	Work tends to drift towards adult agendas and pedagogies of control.
Creativity is valued and seen as something that is intrinsic.	Uniformity often results as young people strive to make the grade or fit a particular model.
Experience is valued, irrespective of what that experience leads to.	Performance is crucial and personal expeiences play second fiddle to achievement of standards and objectives. Work is about achieving something and this is an end in itself.
Work is developed in a contextual way, which takes account of local and group culture.	Programmes, projects and initiatives are copied from others and franchised.

Unpredictability is expected and valued.	Control is paramount to success.
Uniqueness and the recognition of the individual at the centre of the approach is important.	Approaches are designed for mass cohorts and conformity is inbuilt.
Serendipity is likely.	Targets are implicit.
Evolution is inevitable.	Conclusions are defined.

Some brief examples may help to illustrate the difference between these approaches further.

A youth group undertakes some drama work. The process is about the good time the young people have in the drama workshop; the fun they have in writing the script, wearing the costumes, learning how to play, practise and work together. A product-oriented approach will only value the end product – in this case, the actual performance. Those with this bias may ignore all the other benefits of the activity if the final performance did not achieve the required standard.

A worker organizes a meeting of church young people at a local coffee shop to talk about the Bible. She encourages the young people to choose the coffee shop themselves, order the drinks, collect the money, pay for the drinks, choose the Bible passage to discuss, set the questions and determine what should happen next. This process-oriented approach will understand that the success of the meeting is as much about the process of undertaking it as about the quality of the things learned in the Bible study.

The youth work team leader sets each of the team members a task. He asks them to design a series of meetings on the subject of 'justice'. They are instructed not to use any material from Christian books, magazines, DVDs or web sites. Everything they come up with has to be original and appeal to a wide variety of learning styles. The young people themselves must be consulted about the material.

This process-orientated approach is likely to increase the skills, creativity, knowledge, understanding and application of the other workers. A product-orientated team leader is more likely to want to buy the latest book of 'youth work ideas' or 'ready-to-use-meeting' plan so that every worker has material to hand with minimum preparation requirements.

The youth group are going to a worship event at a regional church gathering. The process-orientated worker is as passionate about the informal conversations, discussions and learning that will take place in the minibus on the way there and back as she is about the actual event. The product-orientated worker is likely to consider the evening a success only if the event meets their expectations.

These examples are polarized for illustrative purpose. The rationale, however, is key if we are to ensure that our youth work has a holistic, integrated approach and empowers young people to take responsibility themselves. Recent high-profile social-action projects have not been shown to have had memorable long-term impacts upon the communities where they have taken place. They have, however, had a significant impact upon the young people who took part in them.[2] They are excellent examples of initiatives where the processes are more significant than the products. The process of journeying with young people to assist their personal, social and spiritual development needs to take precedence over the tyranny of outcomes-based approaches or an equally destructive attitude of trying to do youth work with the minimum of thought, effort and preparation.

The tension between process and product is currently very evident within secular youth work where a huge emphasis on outcomes has emerged over the past years. Negative, high-profile media stories about young people have been followed by government initiatives. For instance, stories about knife crime,

gun crime, drug abuse, paedophiles and child protection matters have been followed by legislation, grant programmes, new
projects and initiatives. While action is often necessary, this
'chasing the tail' approach to social policy is fundamentally
flawed and risks focusing on the symptoms rather than seeking
to address the causes of the problems.[3] Many of these government programmes are extremely valuable but because they pursue product they can end up being short-lived and funding-
driven.

We would encourage youth workers to plan, to have effective
strategies and to look for outcomes. However, we would want to
see this done hand in hand with a focus on process and with a
flexible, person-centred, participative and empowering approach
that builds relationally within communities on a long-term basis.
As Bellous reminds us, 'Faith is a moving target.'[4] As such, the
Christian life should be a process of discovery in which we seek
out God as he moves from here to there.

If churches are to work effectively with young people
post-Christendom, they need to understand and practise a
process-oriented approach. It is encouraging to see Jesus epito-
mizing this kind of ministry. His interactions with his disciples,
his followers, the crowds and his critics championed process-
orient-ated qualities. He never sought to control others but
rather gave free choice and sometimes watched as people chose
to leave rather than to follow.[5] His life-sharing approach to discipleship encouraged his followers to experience self-discovery,
develop understanding, and undertake practical application
and experiment in combination with a sense of the mysterious
and the miraculous. He lived a life that was dedicated to seeing
others take up the challenge of building the kingdom. We have
already referred to the pilgrimage and journeying undertaken
by the heroes of the faith who followed in the steps of Jesus and
his example should provide a helpful foundation for any work
with young people undertaken in a church context. To reinforce
some of these ideas and principles, perhaps it would be better
to speak of 'learning Jesus' (process) rather than 'knowing
Jesus' (product).[6]

Growing Church as a Process

Earlier, we considered the HUP and ways in which this might provide a helpful focus when undertaking mission among young people post-Christendom. The logical conclusion to the HUP is the formation or emergence of homogenous church. One example of such a development is the Church on the Edge project.[6]

Church on the Edge

We have already highlighted the fact that Sunday services in most churches, though open to everyone, are aimed primarily at the existing adult church congregation. Churches may seek and claim to be open and inclusive, but often they do not feel that way to those from a different cultural background. Church on the Edge, headed up by Richard Passmore, has sought to engage with this issue, not only in terms of an inclusive theology, but also in seeking to explore questions of 'being' rather than doing.[7]

Most church plants take their DNA from their planting church – often intentionally.[8] Richard, when looking at models of growing church, undertook a straw poll among those that had sought to plant into estates and found that they had struggled, mainly because the culture of the sending church tended to be middle class. Church on the Edge began with the question, 'How do you do church in a way that is genuinely missionary, and has mission in its DNA?' It seemed from the outset that rather than planting out of an existing congregation, the answer was to grow a church from scratch, thus creating a new DNA.

The process for Church on the Edge is based on principles of detached youth work, which provide the background thinking to the whole approach.[9] Although Richard and others have engaged successfully in detached work for a number of years, calling the outcome of their work 'church' would have been unacceptable to the broader church up until relatively recently. Emerging Church and Fresh Expressions have now made this more palatable to the broader Christian constituency. The stages of the process were as follows.

Contacting community in different ways. As well as undertaking detached work with young people, Richard turned his front garden into a vegetable patch to create more opportunities for conversation with his neighbours.

Growing community through mutual acceptance, regular support, trips for young people.

Connecting community. This is the stage at which it might be said that church is formed. Here, there is a reframing of baptism as the traditional point of entry into church. Instead of being baptized, young people go through a rite of passage and are then involved in exploring what it means to be a Christian.

Exploring community through storytelling and the connecting of these stories together.

Ecclesial community through being church together.

Having worked with one group for six months only to lose contact with them, Church on the Edge began working with a second group of skaters, bladers and bikers. At the time of writing, this work is about a year old and has already gone through the first two stages described above. Working regularly in a detached setting with the group, team members have engaged in conversation with the young people and undertaken trips, and projects such as getting lights in place in the local skate park. As the relationships grew, the team began to raise the issue of church explicitly, asking the young people if they would be willing to make the journey to discover what church would mean and look like for them.

As the young people agreed, it was important to help them find a language to describe where and how they saw God in their situation. The term 'flow' was a term they already used to describe the feeling they got when they were skating and, identifying this as a spiritual experience, Richard began to make connections with this sense of 'flow' and God's presence.

Finding key young people within the group who were willing to dialogue about 'flow' took the relationships deeper and gave opportunities to begin to explore issues of spirituality and church. Here, the fact that the young people had no preconceptions was a distinct advantage as the conversations could be genuinely exploratory and open-ended. Richard used stories of the Celtic saints as examples of spirituality, and these appeared to connect with the young people and provide further signposts forward.

Some kind of rite of passage had always been seen as a key part of the process for those who wished to engage explicitly with the exploration of Christianity. In rite of passage stories, leaving behind where they were, heroes set out to meet and battle with their enemies, returning accepted and endorsed by the community. The rite of passage for this group will be a skate pilgrimage to Cornwall. As we write, this pilgrimage is still in the planning stage. The three key young people involved in dialoguing about this are keen that only those who are genuine skaters and really in the 'flow' should be allowed to come. Interestingly, they are also keen to involve others who do not skate but who 'flow' in their own fields – guitar playing and biking. Currently around ten young people will be taking part.

Much preparation has been done, with the team using the metaphor of journey quite consistently to enable the group to engage with spiritual issues, this theme having been present in previous, shorter trips. The pilgrimage will continue to use the skating metaphor, taking the sense of journey and using the image of skate ramps to explore ideas of crossing over from one stage of relationship to another. The young people are aware that by coming along on the skate pilgrimage they are choosing to move from simply being involved in a youth project to researching with the team what church might look like for them.

Practically speaking, the pilgrimage will involve visiting a number of Celtic crosses in Cornwall and seeing what emerges. After the skate pilgrimage, the group will begin to explore together what it means to be church. A group of volunteers has already begun to meet on Sundays and the young people will join them after the skate pilgrimage. The intention is to use stories, parables and non-book discipleship tools to assist dialogue and exploration.

Interestingly, the project has proved very attractive to unchurched adults, several of whom have already expressed an interest in being part of it and helping out. One man, who is now taking on the responsibility of being treasurer, is happy to be involved in the Sunday group because there is no fixed agenda.

Richard is aware that the project might develop in all kinds of ways. The hope is that because what emerges should be a very missional community, other young people will not have to go through the whole process, but will join in at the third stage. This, therefore, has the potential of being a redemptive process for the community of skaters, bladers and bikers, and of then also being genuinely open to the wider community. This development would clearly challenge some traditional thinking around HUP principles, but would show how an approach that began with the HUP could develop to be more inclusive.

Church on the Edge highlights some key ideas that helpfully inform our consideration of church youth work post-Christendom.

- The project has at its heart a commitment to good youth work practice and is founded on solid youth work principles.
- It is process-oriented and begins the journey where the young people are rather than expecting them to fit existing models and structures.
- It is participative and empowering in its approach, engaging fully with the questions the young people have about spirituality.
- It seeks to help young people identify where God is already at work in their lives and find a language to describe this that reflects their culture.

The possibility has been acknowledged that this may be a temporary community because of the stages of growth and development, and the inevitable changes that take place in adolescence. It may be mono-cultural, but equally has the potential to engage with other subcultures or provide a model for other settings such as Toddler Church on the Edge.

The concept of church continues to be contentious for many who are involved in youth work post-Christendom and are struggling to engage young people in existing ecclesiastical structures. In Church on the Edge, much of what church is assumed to be has been put on one side and there is a freedom to explore what church might mean for one particular group. However, it is clear that many of us simply do not have the luxury of starting from scratch. Most youth workers, whether full-time or part-time, paid or volunteer, enthusiastic or reluctant, find themselves in situations where they are undertaking work with young people against the backdrop and within the context of existing church structures, cultures and expectations.

As we acknowledge the lessons that can be drawn out of the exploratory and emerging work of Church on the Edge, we move on to consider how some of these principles might be applied to work with young people within existing church structures.

Working Within the Existing Church

Many youth workers are committed to their churches and the friendships they have within the church. Some have a strong sense of loyalty to a denomination or stream; some are employed or financially supported by a church or group of churches. Yet many find themselves carrying a sense of frustration on behalf of the young people they serve, and often on their own behalf, too. In trying to bridge the widening gap between young people within their culture, and church structures and culture, youth workers can find themselves in a place of tension in which they can often feel that they are being stretched almost to breaking point.

The issues are by no means straightforward and we are aware of the danger of oversimplification. Youth workers and young people are individuals and there are no hard and fast rules. Some of the things we would think wouldn't work appear to be remarkably effective in particular contexts, and some approaches that would seem to have the potential to work brilliantly don't. Nevertheless, for those working within the setting of a declining institution, and caught between the 'now' and the 'not yet', it is important to find some effective ways of working with young people.

In *Church After Christendom*, Stuart Murray highlights five components that make churches worth joining and staying in:

- being open-edged and engaging with contemporary culture;
- nurturing authentic friendships and healthy community;
- cultivating an earthed spirituality where people encounter God;
- holding deep convictions but being unfazed by questions and doubts;
- stimulating faith development at every stage on the journey.[10]

These provide a helpful framework within which to structure our thoughts about church youth work post-Christendom. However, we would wish to add a further quality – that the work should be participative, inclusive and empowering.

Being Open-Edged and Engaging with Contemporary Culture

Church is another country. They do things differently there.'[11]

We have already highlighted the huge gulf between the world inhabited by young people and the culture of most churches, and have acknowledged the dualism that can arise as a result. One of the key tensions faced by youth workers is the way in which many adults brought up in the Christendom era have absolutely no understanding of how 'different' church culture feels to young people. The assumptions made by many adults can be alienating for youth workers – never mind young people.

The church meeting was over. James (16) had been playing guitar in the worship band. Now he and his girlfriend were kissing down at the front of the church. The pastor was furious and asked them to stop behaving inappropriately in 'the house of God'. They couldn't understand what his problem was.

Kelly (17), who is a trainee leader in a youth congregation, wouldn't think twice about going out with someone who wasn't a Christian. She would have to think far more carefully about going out with someone who was a Christian.

Values that would have been widely accepted in the Christendom era are often now perceived by young people as old-fashioned and out-of-date. In some churches there are marked differences between the generations in terms of value base – what is commonly felt to be acceptable and what is not. Issues of dualism are a real problem for many church-going young people. Stacey, who is 18, describes herself as being 'two different people'. She is highly committed to Jesus, is involved in leadership in her youth group – planning and leading worship meetings – and is enthusiastic about sharing her faith. However, she openly describes herself as a completely different person when she is with her non-Christian friends. For her, the gap between church and 'real life' is too large to bridge. Often, this gulf can make it impossible for young people to take their faith into the classroom. It's as if they leave their life in God at the church or youth group door and assume a different identity with which they can survive in school or wherever they spend their days.

In a culture in which they can change their user names on MSN or their pictures on Facebook at the click of a key, many young people do not find a tension in holding a 'dual' identity. In the post-Christendom era, the sense of a flexible approach to identity is pervasive. The postmodern 'plastic self' is 'flexible, amenable to infinite reshaping, according to mood, whim, desire and imagination'.[12] We need to help young people identify where God can be seen or found at work or school or wherever they spend their everyday lives. We need to listen to them, value their experience and help them connect their everyday experience with the God we love and serve. Taking young people's experience as a starting point in exploring issues, rather than beginning with a Bible verse or passage, can be helpful here, as can ensuring that prayer with young people is earthed in the reality of their everyday experience.

As those seeking to assist young people in bridging this gap, we need to take seriously the world that they live in. Jesus used the stuff of the day to connect with those he spent time with. His stories about fishing, sowing seed and looking for sheep would have resonated with his listeners. Unfortunately, many of us are still using his stories rather than finding ways of contextualizing them into today's culture.

David Kinnaman, who has spent years studying young adults' perceptions of Christianity within and outside the church in the United States, highlights the challenges posed to Christian young people by the fact that the issues they face in their choice-laden, everyday world are simply ignored in the majority of churches.[13]

For many young people, even an acknowledgement of the world that they live in helps them to engage with what is being said. Examples and stories that reflect their lives and interests can make a huge difference in enabling them to connect. We have noticed young people's ears prick up in church when something like MSN or Facebook has been mentioned, or when a story has been told about a young person in school or college. For those churches unwilling to embrace broader change, even small things like this can have some effect.

Another factor, which may sound obvious, is the importance of showing an interest in young people's everyday lives. Sometimes church and even youth work can focus on young people's spiritual development at the expense of any consideration of other aspects of their growth. If young people are only asked about spiritual things, the message they receive is that the rest of their lives has little to do with Christianity. They need to be inspired to a passionate life in God – yet not a passion that is dislocated from their everyday life, but a passion that integrates and affirms their existence in school, in college, in work, with friends.

Using contemporary culture to explore issues and engage with discussion is another helpful way of bridging the gap. Many youth workers already use film clips, contemporary music and technology to very good effect. Helping young people hear the voice of God within their own culture provides connecting points, which can assist a sense of integration. Issues of dualism are not helped, however, by pandering to contemporary culture in a way that seeks to replicate or recreate what is 'out there'.

Churches have often tried to copy contemporary culture in order to attract young people. The danger is that this can encourage the kind of consumerism that smacks of an attractional Christendom, instead of an incarnational, approach. When consumerism and celebrity culture are combined with Christendom values, then we can be in big trouble. We cease to be a marginal movement; we over-concentrate on how things look; think short-term; get focused on the latest idea, believing that it will deliver revival and solve all our problems; decide that marketing is the solution to getting young people to church and church-type events; and end up opting for ready-made packages and solutions rather than authentically produced contextual approaches.

Big events have their place, but an attractional focus can increase dualism rather than discourage it because it can allow young people to be detached observers of faith rather than creators of ministry, and encourage them to avoid any responsibility to engage with what is being said from the front, but rather consume it and forget it as they would any piece of entertainment. That is not to say that we should not seek excellence or that we should not use technology or culture, but these should be part of a contextualized approach that really engages with and empowers young people.

Nurturing Authentic Friendships and Healthy Community

So how do we contextualize authentically? Here relationships are key. The importance of relationships within youth work contexts has long been acknowledged, but must be emphasized explicitly in exploring youth work post-Christendom. In a culture that is increasingly networked and in which relationships are tremendously important for young people, it is helpful to ask how we build and nurture authentic relationships and community in the post-Christendom era.

At certain points in adolescence young people find themselves grappling with questions around identity and faith, which result in tensions in terms of belief and belonging to church. Friendship with peers and adults is one thing that appears to 'hold' young people through these key times. Many young people we know who have become disillusioned with church, Christian culture and even God have 'hung in there' because of the relationships they have had with other young people, youth workers and adults in the broader church. Conversely, those young people who have not had such relationships often appear to be much more vulnerable to disappearing when the inevitable times of doubt and questioning come along.

Two young men we know – Steve and John – have been involved in our church youth work since they were 11 years old. Now in their early twenties and both committed Christians, they have found it virtually impossible to make the transition from youth work to 'adult' church meetings. They occasionally come along on a Sunday morning, but often leave part way through the meeting. They do, however, go along to two small groups connected with church, and the relationships within these groups have provided a significant ongoing point of contact. To them, these groups are church; they are the only church they connect with.

One of these groups is for lads their age, another is a totally mixed, apparently random, group of people aged between 17 and 60, who have all, for whatever reason, found themselves on the edge of church. Neither of these groups is particularly spectacular in terms of leadership, content and style. They are ultra simple in their approach, focusing on care for one another, some very 'light' Bible study or discussion, and prayer for one another. Much space is given to relationship building and social activities and it is this that has proved invaluable in creating a context in which Steve and John can feel a sense of belonging and acceptance.

Examples like this, which illustrate the power of community, seem to fly in the face of some of the observations we made about HUP earlier in this book and appear to contradict commonly held beliefs about what young people see as important. Indeed, in some cases, interaction with adults appears to be a really significant part of young people's desire to be in church. One minister, who leads a Baptist church in a rural context, told us about families moving away from the small community-based village church to a large charismatic church in the city. A number of months later, two young people from different families asked to return to the Baptist church. Although the youth work in the city centre church was vibrant, trendy and attended by a large number of young people, they found it difficult to feel a part of it. When asked why they had wanted to return, one of their main reasons was that no adults had spoken to them in the city church. In the village church they experienced a sense of community that somehow helped them feel connected. This experience is echoed in other stories we have heard.

Mandy was 14, and had never had any contact with church until one January when she started bringing her younger sister along to a church youth club. Initially, she would sit out of sight behind screens by the door. Gradually, the youth team got to know her, simply chatting to her casually and then seeking to involve her in what was going on by asking her to help with small tasks such as giving out biscuits.

A number of months later, a youth worker had the opportunity to talk to Mandy's mum, who told her that this was the first group that Mandy's younger sister had ever been willing to go to. Mandy was now a helper and was given a certificate for being a volunteer. That summer she had 80 per cent attendance at school and had been every day for the past 30 days. She had attended school more that term than in the whole of the previous year. She shouts across the playground now and runs over and hugs members of the team when she sees them.

Mandy has not had a glamorous conversion experience, indeed, the team are not sure exactly where she is on her faith journey, but she is on a journey. She is reading the New Testament in magazine format and hers is often the loudest 'amen' in team meeting prayers. Her confidence levels have grown and she now takes part in games, gets gunged and covered in water and listens to stories wide-eyed along with the children in the group. Her journey has been significantly influenced by a sense of being involved and included.

It is important to consider how we enable young people to be part of community – not in a pressured way, but so that they know that they are welcome and wanted. The media give young people such negative press that they often come across as a bit of a liability, unwanted and unwelcome. As the people of God, we should be modelling something different. Church should be a place where young people have opportunities to make a difference, where their presence and contribution are valued and affirmed and where it is clear they would be missed if they were not there.

It is vitally important to give time to young people – to share our lives with them. One of the key ways in which the gap between church and 'life' can be closed is through relationship. If young people are to engage in whole-life faith, then they will need to see examples of what this looks like. In our experience, they need relational places where they can see this faith in action. This demands time and energy.

The professionalization of youth work can sometimes appear to create a tension for those of us who are committed to a whole-life approach to ministry. We would want to emphasize the importance of boundaries. Those working with young people need time off, and need to work safely and responsibly, taking account of Safeguarding and other policies. Within these boundaries, however, we also have to find ways of sharing our lives with, and giving meaningful, relational time to young people.

Simple things such as meeting young people for coffee or, if child protection issues allow, inviting young people to share in family meals, can break down barriers. We have benefited significantly from being part of others' extended families, and whether or not young people come from a Christian family, it is invaluable for them to experience life in another family, whatever its shape and size. There can be challenges for single workers here, but by thinking creatively and working collaboratively it is possible to create opportunities for informal meetings while still maintaining high standards of good, safe practice.

Many churches talk about intergenerational church when they actually mean intergenerational meetings. Social events that will engage with young people are more helpful than almost anything else for breaking down the boundaries between generations. It is important to ensure, however, that these events are young-person friendly. Experience suggests that while swimming is often a non-starter because of many young people's self-consciousness about their bodies, most activities that involve food tend to be popular. Very often, the things that make the difference are not huge and complicated, but rather simple and straightforward, such as adults just talking to young people as equals, learning their names, showing interest in them and valuing them.

In this post-Christendom era, we need to rediscover a sense of simplicity in some of our youth work. More than clever programmes or innovative strategies, young people need adults who are 'like friends', who will sit with them and listen to them for as long as is needed, who will accept them as they are, without feeling the necessity to give them the 'party line' on any and every issue, but who will care enough to challenge and provoke them, to ask the difficult questions and create safe spaces where they can grow and learn and develop as whole people.[14] They need adults who will journey with them long-term and model what it means to follow Jesus in the nitty-gritty challenges of everyday life.

Cultivating an Earthed Spirituality Where Young People Encounter God

In a culture that treats religion and particularly Christianity with scepticism, the importance of encouraging young people to engage with faith in an authentic manner cannot be over-emphasized. Our soup analogy on page 51 recognizes that within the broader culture there is a desire to return to foods that 'feel' authentic. Yet at the same time there appears to be an unprecedented acceptance of the superficial and fake. Young people have a love-hate relationship with authenticity. While they appear happy to tolerate and even celebrate the fake within popular culture, in their relationships and communities they value the authentic.

Conversations with young people have revealed that they have quite high expectations of the people who work with them and who they look up to. One word that has occurred many times is 'hypocrite'. Often young people express disappointment that adults are not always perfect. It sometimes appears to come as a shock that youth workers struggle, fail and occasionally get things wrong. Maybe the message communicated in some circles promotes the idea that Christians are perfect people. While we serve a perfect God, most of us are on a journey that has twists and turns and ups and downs. Perhaps we would do well to remember as we talk with young people that life is often a struggle and it is okay to mess up now and again. In saying this, we are reminded again of how important it is to be incarnational in our work with young people.

David Boyle suggests that something is authentic if it is:

- ethical
- natural
- honest

- simple
- un-spun
- sustainable
- beautiful
- rooted
- human.[15]

This exciting list may provide a value base from which to undertake church youth work.

There appears to be a tendency within some contexts for youth workers to be so overwhelmed by certain models and approaches that they seek to import them wholesale into the context of their local ministry. But experience shows that young people who will rave about an event such as Soul Survivor will be scathing in their criticism if the youth worker tries to replicate it locally. Young people are far more tolerant of simple sessions that are led by their friends. If they are leading something themselves, the criticism is far less and the levels of engagement far higher than for more polished events led by youth workers. One youth worker spoke about a group that had been set up once a month for older teens during the preach slot of the Sunday church service. It was very different from other aspects of the youth work, with no technology and a simple use of well-facilitated discussion. The response of the young people had surprised her as they had engaged wholeheartedly and animatedly in discussions about subjects that were relevant to them.

Creating a culture within our youth work where young people are encouraged to engage with God personally is key here. One group of young people we talked to spoke of the importance to them of actually experiencing God through prayer and ministry in small groups and one to one. The one thing they highlighted as positive in the Sunday services they attended was the opportunity for ministry at the end of the services.

Creating sacred space

We've talked about location and space in the context of resources, but we should add to this that there are different kinds of space. As well as physical space, the spiritual and emotional climate we create is very important. The diverse preoccupations of today's culture clamour for attention more loudly than in any previous culture. Multi-tasking has become an art form as young people watch television, send and receive texts, download music and chat online, often simultaneously, often in their own bedrooms and often while doing their homework. Occasions and times that in previous generations provided space for thinking and reflection – the walk to school, journeys in cars, buses or trains, sitting in the dentist's waiting room – are now, thanks to technological advances, simply further opportunities to communicate or be entertained. One distinctive thing we can do, therefore, within our Christian youth work is carve out space for young people to be still and silent and meet with God.

Youth workers can sometimes be reluctant to allow such space, often feeling under pressure to provide activity-packed programmes that seek to be as engaging and entertaining as the culture young people are used to. Resisting this pressure may be difficult. Sometimes it will demand a gradual change in 'group' culture. Young people who are accustomed to constant activity may find it difficult at first to be still, but the rewards appear to outweigh the challenges.

In one conversation with a group of young people aged 11 to 13, the need for space to be still and quiet was brought home very strongly. When asked what helped them connect with God and learn about him most effectively, they talked about a midweek group they attended. The group leader always gave five or ten minutes of space towards the end of the session for the young people to sit in silence and think about what they had looked at. This time of silence was cited by virtually all the young people as one of the highlights of the time together.

This desire for simplicity is reflected in the resurgence of more traditional, and in some cases ancient, approaches to spirituality. Mark Yaconelli has explored in some depth the importance of rediscovering contemplative approaches to youth ministry[16] and Stuart Murray suggests taking and contextualizing resources drawn from pre-Christendom times, which 'do not carry the Christendom virus that traditions from later centuries do'.[17]

A number of youth workers we know are effectively using these kinds of approaches to good effect in their work with young people in a church context, and there are some good resources available to assist those wishing to experiment with them.[18] A youth worker based in an Anglican church in Sheffield says that she has found meditations and visualization techniques very helpful in working with groups of Christian young people. The young people in her church group prefer these approaches to noisier styles of prayer as they provide opportunities for them to chill out and have their own space. They also appear to help the young people relax and be receptive to hearing God. Examples of activities that have worked particularly well with her group include the following:

- Ignatian style meditations, which encourage young people to visualize themselves as a character in a Bible story. This allows them to consider different perspectives on the event.
- A series of meditations on the seasons of nature. Here the young people used their imaginations to think about the life cycles of plants in connection with the seasons and experiences within their own lives. This was combined with a nature walk.
- The use of extracts from the Benedictine rule of life to consider ways of living and being with other people and to explore issues around behaviour from a spiritual perspective.

It should be noted that youth workers using these approaches need to be aware of the importance of creating a safe emotional space in which to undertake these kinds of activities. Clear boundaries must be set and care taken to avoid any kind of emotional or spiritual manipulation. It is important for young people to know that they can opt out or leave at any time. The youth worker who described the meditations given above feels strongly that her knowledge of the group is vitally important in terms of being aware of issues that might be particularly painful for the young people and might need to be avoided. Youth workers need to exercise particular caution if they are using some of these approaches with groups they do not know.

We have already highlighted the importance of providing opportunities for young people to connect what they are experiencing of God with their everyday lives. This cannot be emphasized too strongly. If faith is to be more than just a 'Sunday' or 'youth group' faith, then constantly identifying how what is being learned relates to everyday life is of crucial importance. Finding other ways of connecting – for example, setting up prayer networks through mobile phones or the internet – can also be helpful.

Being Participative, Inclusive and Empowering

Thinking around authenticity and engaging with God links very closely with participation, inclusivity and empowerment. Not only are these three issues key principles of professional youth work,[19] they are also vital if our ministry with young people is to be effective.

In their leisure activities, young people have more opportunities than ever before to 'create' the worlds in which they live. In the area of technology in particular, be it gaming, communication or buying and selling, they are presented with endless choice and opportunity. The world of church can, by comparison, appear rigid and inflexible. Models of leadership within church culture often still propagate top-down, hierarchical approaches, which can discourage any meaningful participation in decision-making and shaping of the work. Most adults, never mind young people, often take the role of consumers within church contexts. There can be a tension here for youth workers who are keen to work participatively and are seeking to empower young people.

A reluctance to empower does not appear to be reflected in the life and ministry of Jesus. A glance through the gospels shows us a leader who was quick to celebrate success, see opportunity and release potential among those he lived alongside. If he lived and worked in this way today, he would be clearly demonstrating good youth work practice in some key areas:

- including children and young people (Lk. 18:15–17);
- promoting participation (Mt. 12:46–50);
- equipping and spending time mentoring and discipling (Mk. 7:17; 9:2,30–31);
- empowering and releasing (Mt. 10);
- giving responsibility (Jn. 13; 16).

Much has been written about participation, inclusiveness and empowerment in youth work and it is helpful to highlight some examples of how this can work effectively in a church context.

Liam (16) had never really been that involved in the church youth work, but returned from a Christian camp very keen to do something for God. The midweek youth meeting had been moved to a Sunday evening, so he decided to set up a cell group that would meet on a Wednesday evening. The format was very simple – Bible study, followed by prayer and worship. One of the youth workers popped in to support it, but Liam and his friends facilitated the whole evening.

Becky (18) and Shannon (15) lead a youth worship event once a month at their church. Although they've been given a completely free rein, their youth worker finds it interesting that they tend to use the same format as the 'adult' church they go to, with a time of worship followed by a preach. The preach is much shorter than in the adult service and there's freedom for anyone to interrupt who wants to – people often do, to ask questions or clarify something. They tend to use very creative approaches to prayer and are keen to create their own space – they don't have chairs on principle, as that makes it feel 'different'. They have adult support in terms of the music and they are seeing a number of adults and younger brothers and sisters coming along as well as the young people themselves.

What these examples illustrate is that participation and empowerment do not have to be huge or glamorous. Often it is in the very ordinary aspects of church and youth group life that young people want and need space to be involved. In all these cases, youth workers have given space and provided support where needed. In some months – when the young people have had exams, for example – they have had to give additional support. For those struggling to engage with more participative approaches, there are some really innovative methodologies, with those such as World Café[20] and Open Space Technology[21] offering some interesting starting points.

Holding Deep Convictions but Being Unfazed by Questions and Doubts

Several development theories have highlighted adolescence as a time of questioning and exploring. In his work on socio-emotional development, Erik Erikson identifies the years from 12 to 15 as those when young people are seeking to resolve issues around their own identity, a process that inevitably involves much questioning, some element of crisis and the reconciliation of diverse roles.[22] James Fowler, in his work on faith development, highlights the challenges that young people can experience as they seek to move from a conforming faith that is chosen and owned by others to a first-hand faith.[23]

The questions, doubts and tensions that emerge for young people during this time are exacerbated by both the experience-driven nature of the broader culture and the apparent dogmatism of much of the church. On the surface at least, contemporary culture appears to run by the mantra, 'If it feels right, it must be right.' Sometimes, because of this prevailing culture, churches feel the need to be even stronger on absolutes and can consequently appear to young people to be stuck in a time warp, having little to say that helpfully informs the challenges they face in their everyday lives. We know a number of young people who have hit seasons of doubt and questioning and have found no relational spaces within church in which to explore these questions effectively.

It is important to highlight the fact that 'certainties' may appear very attractive to young people who find themselves adrift in a culture that is completely ignorant of the Christian faith. Some young people we meet want answers and are frustrated by youth work that appears wishy-washy and doesn't deliver absolutes. It is important for individual youth workers to be sensitive to the needs of the young people they are working with and to be aware of the stage of development they are in. Sometimes there is a need for contextualized and relevant biblical teaching that can give young people the confidence to make clear choices during the difficult school years. At other times the youth worker will need to respond appropriately to questions and doubts.

Killen and de Beer's work on theological reflection provides a very helpful framework that youth workers may wish to consider as they seek to find an approach that is both balanced and biblical.[24] They speak of three different places from which we can 'do' theology. First, the 'place of certainty', which draws wholly upon Christian tradition, is strong on absolutes and uses chapter and verse of the Bible to justify clear pronouncements on any and every issue. This is the place that would be most visible in strongly evangelical contexts.

At the opposite end of the spectrum, there is the 'place of self-reliance', which would be more reflective of contemporary culture. Here, experience is the loudest voice and pragmatism the order of the day. What 'works for me' is the key issue. This is the place that most young people in today's culture would tend to go to.

Killen and de Beer argue that to engage in theological reflection effectively, we must find a middle ground, a 'place of exploration', where Christian tradition and personal experience are allowed to connect and converse together in order to find a way forward. For youth workers post-Christendom, this appears to be a helpful approach. It encourages us to retain our deep convictions and draw on biblical truth and Christian tradition, yet challenges us to engage with the issues that young people face as they struggle with the integration of faith and life. In order to wrestle with these tensions, a good foundation of biblical knowledge is essential. It is no good seeking to draw from a scriptural tradition we are ignorant of. Valuing questions as a key part of the learning process is also essential. We must be willing not to have all the answers.

Youth workers wishing to create a safe 'place of exploration' need to be mature enough to manage their own emotional responses to young people's doubts and questions. The pressure to give a pat response to a question because we feel that that is what the church leadership would want can often be quite strong. There can also be a sense of anxiety if a young person appears very negative about the youth work, the church or even God. In allowing young people space to express themselves and feel accepted within their questioning, it is important to recognize that this negativity is usually not a personal attack on the youth worker. Good listening skills are key here.

It is also important to mention that those working with young people need to be wise if they themselves are going through a time of questioning and doubt. However tempting it may be to use the youth group as a personal place of exploration, this is singularly inappropriate.

Stimulating Faith Development at Every Stage on the Journey

We have already highlighted the way in which church increasingly finds itself competing on the margins alongside other recreational activities.[25] For many young people, particularly those in middle-class areas, church is simply one among a large number of activities that they engage with in their spare time. In a culture that values academic achievement, faith-based interests may come much farther down the list than school activities. Parents may be reluctant to let their children out for midweek events, and at the weekend, Christian groups are often competing directly with activities that have a much more immediate appeal.

A further challenge post-Christendom is the way in which trends of church attendance have affected the experience of young people brought up in Christian families. Stuart Murray addresses the issue of those who believe but don't belong and those who believe but belong intermittently, or less intensely than they used to.[26] Many of those in Generation X who have left church or only attend sporadically have a firm foundation in the Christian faith. Indeed, Alan Jamieson's research draws attention to the fact that many of those pursuing faith outside the church have previously been involved in mission and had leadership roles in churches.[27] The challenge for the children of these church-leavers is that there is a pervasive and erroneous assumption within the church that they have the same foundation of biblical understanding and knowledge as their parents.

It is against this backdrop that church-based youth groups are working. If they are to be effective, they must take seriously the issue of discipleship and consider how young people might be equipped to live as disciples of Christ in a culture that is ignorant of, and in many cases culturally hostile to, the gospel.

Our conversations with young people and youth workers have highlighted a number of further factors that hinder young people's learning and growth in church-based contexts. The issue of Sunday meetings or services appears to be a consistent concern in a broad range of churches. Young people, although expected to attend, appear to get very little out of these services. In terms of what doesn't work for young people, there are a number of recurring themes:

- adult expectations, such as sitting still and listening for long periods;
- examples and talks that don't connect with experience;
- being told what to think without opportunities to discuss and explore;
- anything that feels insincere or hypocritical, including tokenistic involvement;
- long sermons or talks;
- entertainment with no substance.

Encouraging young people in their spiritual journeys is no small task and the challenges presented in this cultural context demand responses and approaches that are contextual and holistic. Of great concern from this point of view, and highlighted by many youth workers, are the high levels of biblical illiteracy among young people. It is not that they cannot read, but that they simply do not appear to want to read the Bible. Engaging with this issue provides a starting point but is by no means the end of the story.

Deeper discipleship

If discipleship is to challenge dualism, it must be whole-life focused. To explore how this kind of discipleship learning might take place, we have found it helpful to adapt a model developed for use in adult training contexts.[28] Here, we see that knowledge is a starting point but not an end in itself. If effective learning is to take place, knowledge needs to move on into understanding, then into direct and indirect application and finally into integration.

Knowledge of the Christian story is an important part of the discipleship process. We need to find ways of communicating and retelling God's story to this generation of young people.

Understanding builds on knowledge. Understanding is more than knowing about, it is engaging with and thinking through the Christian story. To understand is to perceive the meaning, cause or significance of something.

Direct and indirect application require making connections between the Christian story and everyday life. Direct application may involve exploring what a particular value or principle might look like fleshed out in practice. What might it mean in school, in college, in work, on the net? What implications does it have for decisions? Indirect application happens when a young person understands an issue deeply enough to apply it in a completely different situation or context.

Integration happens when Christian truth becomes part of the young person's heart and soul. When faith becomes integrated, a young person's attitudes and values begin to change and come in line with the heart and mind of God. Scripture comes alive and doesn't just ring some bells but changes ways of thinking and ways of being. Knowledge has moved from the head and become 'learning by heart' in the true sense.

Regurgitating and reprocessing

Trevor Cooling talks about the difference between regurgitating and reprocessing.[29] This is a helpful way of considering issues of deeper discipleship. If young people are learning something to regurgitate it, it need go no farther than their minds. They can learn it by rote, recite it from memory and deliver it when necessary. Some young people 'know' all the right answers and can give them as needed. Reprocessing, however, involves far more engagement with the material presented. It isn't a case of simply 'playing back' what has been said or done, but rather of taking something, working with it, wrestling with it and bringing it back in a different form. If this process is done effectively, the greater levels of engagement will result in a deeper level of understanding and learning.

If we are to make 'deeper' disciples and get away from the idea of Christianity as 'just another leisure activity', it is essential in our youth work to:

- help young people connect Christian truth with their past and current experiences;

- value their everyday experiences as part of the learning process;
- use multi-sensory approaches that engage the affective (emotions and will) as well as the cognitive (mind);
- acknowledge differences in personality, learning style and types of intelligence in our work and use a range of creative approaches and methods to cater for a broad variety of people;
- find ways of earthing spirituality and grounding it in real life;
- model what we are talking about so that young people 'see' and 'experience' faith in action;
- use technology and contemporary culture where relevant and appropriate;
- be real, participative and encourage ownership of the processes, allowing young people to set agendas, steer conversations and try things out;
- encourage active engagement with God and provide opportunities for prayer, ministry and personal reflection;
- create environments that are accepting, loving, valuing and encouraging;
- involve young people in setting appropriate boundaries and challenge inappropriate behaviour where necessary to create safe spaces where learning can take place.

Approaches to discipleship

Every individual is unique and each young person will undertake the spiritual journey in a slightly different way. We have already highlighted the danger church faces of appearing staid and one dimensional in contrast to the choice-laden postmodern culture, but there is really no reason why youth workers cannot be creative and innovative in the approaches to discipleship that they use.

Many youth workers find that discipleship happens very effectively in groups. Opportunities for young people to gather together and discuss issues with their peers can encourage mutual spiritual development and learning. Peer-led initiatives have proved popular in recent times and provide much-needed opportunities for the kind of ownership, empowerment and participation we mentioned earlier.

Green and Christian have explored the idea of 'accompanying' as an approach to working with young people in a faith-based context. The idea of soul friendship or spiritual direction can be really helpful in this regard. The spiritual director or soul friend is not a guru with all the answers or an infallible problem solver, but rather 'a man or woman of experience, knowledge, and skills' who accompanies another person on their spiritual journey.[30] Encouraging young people to have a spiritual director or soul friend can provide the kind of individual support we have mentioned and has the potential to create a safe relational space for exploration and learning. This approach has similarities with some one-to-one discipleship models but also has clear differences. The spiritual director tends to be less directive and the overall context is very much one of mutual learning and journeying.

Some youth workers may blanch at the idea of spiritual direction for young people, imagining that they would have to do all this themselves. There is no reason why this should be the case. In our experience, many Christians who would not want to run a weekly youth club are happy to spend time with young people in a more low-key role. With the right input and training and an awareness of good practice issues, one-to-one work can bear much fruit.[31] One church linked to a Celtic community is seeking to put spiritual direction in place for all the young people in the church.

In smaller churches or churches where there are not many young people and opportunities to meet in larger groups are fewer and farther between, spiritual direction can provide invaluable support for individuals. In larger churches, even those with thriving youth work, some young people may still find themselves struggling with what is going on and may prefer a one-to-one approach, or the opportunity to meet with another person may provide opportunities to earth, apply and integrate learning that is happening in other contexts.

Closing Thoughts

At lunch following a recent family funeral we overheard one teenager speaking to another about the vicar, who had just arrived.

'What's he doing here?'

'He'll have come for the free lunch.'

It saddened us that in a culture that is largely ignorant of the Christian story, church ministers were still viewed in such a way. We did, however, observe that the vicar spoke to no one under the age of 60 during the whole event. This is the church we are a part of. This is the body to which we belong. But young people need to regain a sense of destiny and we dream of a church that recognizes the part they have to play in the body of Christ. Young people are not faceless groups in hoods, but individuals created in the image of God who have needs, hopes, fears, dreams, aspirations and purpose. They need to be valued as individuals not as anonymous souls within a marginalized group.

We dream of a church that empowers rather than disempowers, that allows young people to share their views, that really listens to them and gives them a voice. We dream of leadership that is participative and collaborative. We dream of a church that supports absurd causes, fights unwinnable battles, prays impossible prayers; a church that resonates with the laughter of the Jesus we see in the gospels – the Jesus who swings children above his head, tickles them and plays games with them during the sermon; the Jesus who upsets the religious, surprises the respectable, welcomes the sinner and the sinned-against.

We still have many questions. Might it be the case that in some situations we may need to enable some churches to have a 'good death' so that something new may emerge? Can the existing church really engage with young people in this post-Christendom era? Can she lay aside her preoccupations and rediscover her first love? And can she begin to dance with this generation of young people instead of sitting frustrated with rows of empty pews, waiting for the young people to come through the doors?

7

And Finally . . .

Over the last couple of years, Bishop Roger Sainsbury has compiled what he calls 'Ten Commandments for Youth Work Today'.[1] These not only provide extremely valuable signposts for effective youth work, they also focus upon the need for clear values and effective processes to underpin, inform, inspire and facilitate work with young people. These commandments are:

1. Listen to the voices of young people.
2. Have a special concern for the socially excluded and disadvantaged.
3. Work co-operatively with other agencies, particularly schools.
4. Give spiritual development a priority.
5. Demonstrate tough love.
6. Offer emotional and spiritual security.
7. Organize activities that help young people feel valued and significant.
8. Challenge the demonization of young people.
9. Help build community cohesion by youth work that educates young people to value our common humanity and shared citizenship, not sectarian hate.
10. Be active politically to seek long-term funding for youth work from national and local government.

We don't intend here to comment upon and unpack each of these commandments. You may find that some resonate with you more than others, and you may wish to spend time thinking through and developing your own ten commandments. It is important, though, to recognize that we all live and work from a value base. Whether or not we are aware of it, our beliefs and values will shape our approach to our work with young people.

Often it appears that Christians are looking for the next 'big thing', the secret solution that will give us the keys we need to reach people with the gospel. Christian youth work often seems to embrace particular trends for a season. If we are not careful, we can lurch from one good idea to the next without really understanding what we are seeking to do. Our prayer for this book is not that it may send you into a fresh spiral of activity, but rather that it may help you to consider prayerfully the work you undertake with young people in the context of a changing culture.

Our experience is that often the changes we need to make are not particularly dynamic or glamorous. In 2 Kings chapter 5, Naaman, an army commander, is seeking a cure for his leprosy. When Elisha tells him to go and bathe seven times in the River Jordan, Naaman is furious. He had expected something far more dramatic and 'spiritual'. Eventually, Naaman's anger subsides and he does what is asked of him, whereupon his leprosy is completely healed. For us, too, the ways forward may not be particularly dramatic or glamorous. We may need to start by acknowledging and working with what we already have . . .

> One of the builders explained that the first thing you need to do on a new site is look at all the resources that are there very carefully. Then try to utilise all the materials that are naturally at hand.[2]

In some cases, God may be encouraging us to get back to some of the simple, basic aspects of youth work. He may ask us to focus on loving young people, accepting them, welcoming them, giving them space and time, or simply creating space where they can encounter Jesus. We may need to lose some of our busyness so we can get to know them and build community with them. We may have to allow and assist them in contextualizing faith for their generation as they discover and grow their ways of worshipping, praying and being church.

Whatever God may require of us in this season, it is likely that we will be challenged by the paradoxes at work in youth work post-Christendom:

- being counter-cultural, yet engaging with culture;
- holding deep convictions, yet being willing to explore and question;
- being earthed and grounded, yet seeking a deeper, Bohemian spirituality;
- creating environments that attract people, yet discouraging consumerism;
- balancing biblical truth with personal experience.

These paradoxes may at first glance seem incompatible, yet as we look at the life of Jesus, we see a man who is able to embrace the apparent tensions of grace and truth, judgement and mercy, faith and works. As we seek to follow Jesus, serve those around us and play our part in building the kingdom of God, may we, too, find a creativity in the tensions of the post-Christendom era, a creativity that enables us to be effective, incarnational and inspirational in our work with young people.

Endnotes

1 – Introduction

[1] Peter G. Brierley, *UK Christian Handbook* (London: Christian Research, 2005); Peter G. Brierley, *Religious Trends No. 5: The Future of the Church* (London: Christian Research, 2005).

[2] LifeWay Research Survey of 1,023 Protestants conducted April and May 2007.

[3] See Sara Savage, Sylvia Collins-Mayo, Bob Mayo and Graham Cray, *Making Sense of Generation Y* (London: Church House Publishing, 2006); Phil Rankin, *Buried Spirituality* (Salisbury: Sarum College, 2005); Jo Pimlott, Nigel Pimlott and Dave Wiles, *Inspire Too!* (Birmingham: Frontier Youth Trust, 2005).

[4] For the sake of simplicity, the terms 'youth work' and 'youth worker' are used throughout to encompass the wide range of work with young people that Christians undertake. This includes youth ministry, youth work, youth pastoring, youth leading, youth and community work and youth outreach work.

[5] Søren Kierkegaard, *Attack Upon Christendom* (Princeton, N.J.: Princeton University Press, 1968), 37.

[6] In cases where young people's stories are quoted, names have been changed.

[7] Stuart Murray, *Post-Christendom* (Milton Keynes: Paternoster Press, 2004).

[8] Murray, *Post-Christendom*, 19.

[9] See Murray, *Post-Christendom*, 20.

[10] Eddie Gibbs and Ryan Bolger, *Emerging Churches: Creating Christian Communities in Postmodern Cultures* (London: SPCK, 2006), 17.

2 – Christendom, Youth Work and Young People

1. Acts 20:7–12.
2. This is not an attack on preaching *per se*, merely a reflection that some people, and especially young people, often have different needs and respond in different ways to some of the things adult Christians take for granted.
3. Savage et al, *Making Sense*.
4. W.R. Daggett, educationalist, cited in the publicity for the Business and Education Summit, October 2006.
5. Patricia Hersch, *A Tribe Apart: A Journey Into the Heart of American Adolescence* (New York/Toronto: Ballantine, 1998), 165.
6. 'What Teenagers Look for in Church', The Barna Group (2007), see www.barna.org.
7. Mike Bishop, 'The Church A Subversive Community', *Next-Wave* (May–June 2002).
8. www.nextreformation.com/wp-admin/leadership/diaspora htm>.
9. Hebrews 4:9.
10. Acts 2:46.
11. Peter Lupson, *Thank God for Football* (Elk Grove, Calif.: Azure Press, 2007).
12. For further exploration of these issues see Ruth Gilchrist, Tony Jeffs and Jean Spence (eds.), *Drawing on the Past: Studies in the history of community and youth work* (Leicester: National Youth Agency, 2006).
13. For example, Birmingham City Council (and many other local authorities) encourage people seeking to combat anti-social behaviour to 'engage faith communities and voluntary organisations in planning to divert young people from offending behaviour'. While perhaps a noble sentiment, this is also a potentially manipulative and exploitative use of the local church or mosque. See 'Reduce Offending, Re-offending and Anti-social Behaviour' at www.birmingham.gov.uk.
14. Michael Frost and Alan Hirsch, *The Shaping of Things to Come: Innovation and Mission for the 21st Century Church* (Peabody, Mass.: Hendrickson, 2003), 13.
15. Kierkegaard, *Attack*, 268–72.
16. See, for example, Murray, *Post-Christendom*, 121.
17. Rob Bell, 'Going to New Places', talk at *Youthwork, the Conference*, Eastbourne, November 2006.

[18] Alan Hirsch, *The Forgotten Ways: Reactivating the Missional Church* (Grand Rapids, Mich.: Brazos Press, 2006), 55–6.

[19] See Pimlott et al, *Inspire Too!*, Chapter 3.

[20] Dave Andrews, *Compassionate Community Work: An Introductory Course for Christians* (Carlisle: Piquant Editions, 2006), 54.

[21] 1988 Education Reform Act.

[22] In one sense, Christian schools are the obvious exemption to this, but even in Christian schools, many of the pupils have no faith or a different faith to that of Christianity.

[23] Janet King, *Leading Worship in Schools: An Open Door for Christians?* (Eastbourne: Monarch Publications, 1990), 31.

[24] Bert Jones and John Rose, 'Early Development of the Youth Service in Wales 1830–1917' in Gilchrist et al, *Essays*, 30.

[25] Frost and Hirsch, *Shape*, 39.

[26] Ryan K. Bolger speaking in Birmingham Cathedral, July 2006, at a meeting held in connection with the Emerging Churches Tour.

[27] Murray, *Post-Christendom*, 203.

[28] Michael Binyon, 'York's local hero – the first Christian emperor', *The Times*, 29 July 2006.

3 – Perspectives on Young People, Life and Spirituality

[1] 'Modern life leads to more depression among children', letter to *The Daily Telegraph*, 12 September 2006.

[2] Julia Margo and Mike Dixon, *Freedom's Orphans: Raising Youth in a Changing World* (London: Institute of Public Policy Research, 2006).

[3] *Respect? – The voice behind the hood* (Youthnet and British Youth Council, July 2006).

[4] Tim Evans and Dave Wiles, *Hope – Stories from the Road* (Birmingham: Frontier Youth Trust/Worth Unlimited, 2007).

[5] Deirdre Fernand, 'Turbo Teens Go On A World Of Conquest', *The Sunday Times*, 7 January 2007.

[6] Margo and Dixon, *Freedom's*.

[7] Francis Gilbert, *Yob Nation* (London: Portrait, 2006).

[8] Centers for Disease Control and Prevention Statistics report (2006).

[9] A UK survey of 1,000 boys and girls aged 7 to 12 found that from a list of five summer holiday activities, 25 per cent said they spent 'most time' playing various types of computer game on their own.

See Michael Howe, 'A Comparative Study of the Effects of Holiday "Brain Resting" Periods on Children's Mental Development', Report of Research for Powergen (September 2001).

[10] See the *National Centre for Social Research Report* published in 2003 by the Department of Health.

[11] *National Health and Nutrition Examination Survey*, 1999–2002 cited on National Center for Health Statistics, US Department of Health and Human Services.

[12] *British Medical Journal* (15 June 2002), 324:1416 from www.bmj.com.

[13] *Mental Health of Children and Young People in Great Britain*, 2004 (Office for National Statistics, 2005); *Children and Adolescent Mental Health* (British Medical Association, 2006).

[14] Prison Reform Trust, 2001.

[15] See Keith Hawton, Karen Rodham and Emma Evans, *By Their Own Young Hand: Deliberate Self Harm and Suicidal Ideas in Adolescents* (London: Jessica Kingsley Publishers, 2006). According to these authors, 11 per cent of 15- and 16-year-old girls self-harm.

[16] Peter G. Brierley, *Reaching and Keeping Tweenagers* (London: Christian Research, 2003).

[17] Sue Budden, Jo Pimlott, Nigel Pimlott, Dave Wiles, *Enabling Participation* (Birmingham: Frontier Youth Trust, 2003).

[18] See Savage et al, *Making Sense*; Rankin, *Buried*; Christian Smith with Melissa Lundquist Denton, *Soul Searching: The Religious and Spiritual Lives of American Teenagers* (New York: Oxford University Press, 2005); Leslie Francis and Mandy Robbins, *Urban Hope and Spiritual Health: The Adolescent Voice* (Werrington: Epworth, 2005); Lat Blaylock, 'Spiritual survey, seventeen year olds – more spiritual than religious, less atheistic than you may have thought', *dare2engage* (September 2005).

[19] Walter Brueggemann, *Spirituality of the Psalms* (Minneapolis: Augsburg Fortress, 2001).

[20] See the work by James Fowler in his *Stages of Faith: The Psychology of Human Development and the Quest for Meaning* (New York: Harper and Row, 1981), and *Faithful Change – The Personal and Public Challenges of Postmodern Life* (Nashville: Abingdon Press, 1996); see also John H. Westerhoff, *Bringing Up Children in the Christian Faith* (Minneapolis, Minn.: Winston Press, 1980); and *Will Our Children Have Faith?* (San Francisco, Calif.: Harper, 1984).

[21] This is explored comprehensively in Steve Bullock and Nigel Pimlott, *Glimpses* (Leicester: National Youth Agency, 2007).

[22] Greenberg Quinlan Rosner research, 'OMG! How Generation Y is Redefining Faith in the iPod Era' (Reboot, Brookings Institute, Washington, April 2005).

[23] This model is widely used. Original source unknown.

[24] Rankin, *Buried*, 43.

[25] Andrew Smith, 'Soapbox', *Youthwork* (November 2006).

[26] Nigel Pimlott, *Faiths and Frontiers* (Birmingham: Frontier Youth Trust, 2001).

[27] Iain Duncan-Smith et al, *Breakdown Britain* (London: Social Policy Justice Group, 2006).

[28] Jane Shilling, 'Two's Company, Three's Antisocial?', *The Times*, 3 August 2006.

[29] Originally so called by Peter Drucker, *The Age of Discontinuity: Guidelines to our Changing Society* (Rutgers University, New Jersey: Transaction Publishers, 1969).

[30] Evans and Wiles, *Hope*, 22.

[31] Margo and Dixon, *Freedom's*, viii.

[32] Duncan-Smith, *Breakdown*, 15.

[33] Graeme McMeekin, 'Youth Justice? But We're Christians', *Perspectives Journal* (Summer 2006), 2.

4 – Reaching Young People Post-Christendom

[1] Kjell Nordstrom and Jonas Ridderstrale, *Funky Business: Talent Makes Capital Dance* (Stockholm: Bookhouse Publishing, 2002), 88.

[2] David Bosch, *Transforming Mission: Paradigm Shifts in the Theology of Mission* (Maryknoll, N.Y.: Orbis, 1991), 390.

[3] For more developed thinking on this, see Richard Passmore, *Off the Beaten Track: A Fresh Approach to Youth Work and Church Based on Jesus' Travels* (Birmingham: Christian Education Publications, 2004).

[4] Dietrich Bonhoeffer, *The Cost of Discipleship* (London: SCM Press, 1959), 129.

[5] www.purposedriven.com/en-US/AboutUs/WhatIsPD/PD_Articles/Fishing.htm.

[6] Donald A. McGavran, *Understanding Church Growth* (Grand Rapids: Eerdmans, 1970), 163.

[7] Richard Harries, *God Outside the Box: Why Spiritual People Object to Christianity* (London: SPCK, 2002), ix.

8 An example of this approach is given in Chapter 6.

9 See, for example, Pete Ward, *Youthwork and the Mission of God: Frameworks for Relational Outreach* (London: SPCK, 1997).

10 Speaking at a conference in Northampton, 6 December 2004.

11 Rankin, *Buried*, 42–50.

12 Harries, *God*, 107–8.

13 www.apexchurch.org.

14 'Stories from the Edge,' www.fyt.org.uk.

15 Sally McFague, *Speaking in Parables*, www.religion-online.org.

16 See 'A Report on the Evaluation of Evangelistic Events in the UK: Manchester 2000; Festival Manchester; Soul in the City – London; MerseyFest and NE1' (commissioned by The Jerusalem Trust, 2007). Available from www.fyt.org.

17 Nick Shepherd, 'Soul in the City – Mission as Package Holiday', Anvil, 22:4 (2005).

18 Kenda Creasy Dean, *Practicing Passion: Youth and the Quest for a Passionate Church* (Grand Rapids: Eerdmans, 2004), 193.

19 Jerusalem Trust, 'Report'.

20 'Stories from the Edge', www.fyt.org.uk.

21 Reproduced from Leonard P. Barnett, *The Church Youth Club* (London: Methodist Association of Youth Clubs, 1951), 49. Accessed from the informal education archives at www.infed.org.

22 Source unknown.

5 – Resourcing Youth Work Post-Christendom

1 Jemma Grieve, Veronique Jochum, Belinda Pratten and Claire Steel, *Faith in the Community: The Contribution of Faith-based Organisations To Rural Voluntary Action* (London: The National Council for Voluntary Organisations, 2007), 19.

2 Martin Saunders, *Youthwork*, July 2007.

3 Tom Horwood, 'Face to Faith', *The Guardian*, 4 August 2007.

4 Horwood, 'Face to Faith'.

5 See http://www.english-heritage.org.uk/inspired/server/show/ConWebDoc.6480.

6 See Peter G. Brierley, *Pulling Out of the Nose Dive* (London: Christian Research, 2006). Most growth appears to be taking place among Pentecostal churches and churches that serve ethnic minority groupings.

[7] 'Some Church of England congregations are thriving. In 2001 some 2,600 parishes (20%) had over one hundred adults attending Sunday services. On the other hand, roughly 800 parishes (6%) had ten adults or fewer worshipping on Sunday, representing an estimated 1,000 church buildings.' Trevor Cooper, 'How do we keep our Parish Churches?' (The Ecclesiological Society, 2004).

[8] See www.tubestation.org.

[9] See also Emlyn Williams, *Reaching and Keeping Volunteers* (Cambridge: Grove Books, 2006); Malcolm Herbert and Sally Nash, *Supervising Youth Workers* (Cambridge: Grove Books, 2006).

[10] It should be emphasized, however, that proper procedures in terms of Criminal Records Bureau checks should be undertaken before allowing people to work as volunteers.

[11] Robert Putnam, *Bowling Alone* (New York: Simon and Schuster, 2001).

[12] *Power of the Postcode*, a national survey for Norwich Union, carried out in Britain by Ipsos, MORI (2006).

[13] See, for example, Acts 2:2; 5:42; 10:23; 16:34; 20:20.

[14] Leonard Sweet, *Postmodern Pilgrims: First Century Passion for the 21st Century Church* (Nashville: Broadman and Holman, 2000).

[15] Barbara and Tom Butler, *Just Spirituality in a World of Faiths* (London: Mowbray, 1996).

[16] See www.remar.org.

[17] This term was coined by Michael Hammer and James Champy, see *Reengineering the Corporation: A Manifesto for Business Revolution* (London: Nicholas Brealey Publishing, 1993).

[18] Data source: *Yahoo! PE Fingertip Facts*, Q1 2007.

[19] See www.facebook.com, www.twitter.com, www.hab-bo.com, www.secondlife.com, www.youtube.com.

[20] See 'Young Canadians in a Wired World', Phase 2 (Ottowa, Ontario: Media Awareness Network, ERIN Research, 2005).

[21] George Pitcher, 'No Leadership from the Church, How about Thought Leadership?', *St Bride's Church Magazine*, July 2007, originally published in *The Daily Telegraph*, 28 May 2007.

[22] See www.bohemiancafe.co.uk for one online attempt to recreate the ethos of the cafés.

[23] Typified by Baz Luhrmann's postmodern interpretation in the film *Moulin Rouge* (20th Century Fox, 2001).

[24] Letter to Mme R.C. de Toulouse-Lautrec, 28 December 1886, cited by Reinhold Heller, *Toulouse-Lautrec: The Soul of Montmartre* (New York: Prestel, 1997), 20.

6 – Church Work Post-Christendom

[1] Adapted from *Collins Pocket Dictionary of the English Language* (London: W. M. Collins, 1981).

[2] Jerusalem Trust, 'Report'.

[3] For a further discussion about this, see Jo and Nigel Pimlott, *Responding to Challenging Behaviour* (Cambridge: Grove Books, 2005).

[4] Joyce E. Bellous in Cathy Ota and Clive Erricker (eds.), *Spiritual Education: Literary, Empirical and Pedagogical Approaches* (Brighton: Sussex Academic Press, 2005), 123.

[5] See, for example, Mt. 19:16–22.

[6] Luke Timothy Jackson, *Living Jesus: Learning the Heart of the Gospel* (New York: HarperCollins, 1999).

[7] Church on the Edge is a formal partnership between Devon and Exeter Diocese, Frontier Youth Trust (FYT) and the Church Mission Society (CMS). For more information and up-to-date blogs, go to www.sundaypapers.org.uk.

[8] For further exploration of this issue, see Bob Jackson's *Encounters on the Edge* series at<www.encountersontheedge.org.uk.

[9] Richard Passmore, *Meet Them Where They're At* (Bletchley: Scripture Union, 2003); and *Beaten*.

[10] Murray, *Church*, 64. For the purpose of this exploration, the order has been changed.

[11] Adapted from L.P. Hartley, *The Go-Between* (London: Penguin Books, 1958).

[12] David Lyon, *Jesus in Disneyland: Religion in Postmodern Times* (Cambridge: Polity Press, 2000).

[13] David Kinnaman and Gabe Lyons, *UnChristian: What a new generation really thinks about Christianity . . . and why it matters* (Grand Rapids, Mich.: Baker Books, 2007).

[14] Kerry Young, *The Art of Youth Work* (Lyme Regis: Russell House, 2006²).

[15] David Boyle, *Authenticity: Brands, Fakes, Spin and the Lust for Real Life* (London: HarperCollins, 2003).

[16] Mark Yaconelli, *Contemplative Youth Ministry: Practising the Presence of Jesus with Young People* (London: SPCK, 2006).

[17] Murray, *Church*, 110.

[18] See, for example, Jenny Baker and Moya Ratnayake, *Tune In, Chill Out* (Birmingham: Christian Education, 2004).

[19] Young, *Art*.

[20] Juanita Brown and David Isaacs, *The World Café: Shaping Our Futures Through Conversations That Matter* (San Francisco, Calif.: Barrett-Koehler, 2004).

[21] Harrison Owen, *Open Space Technology: A User's Guide* (San Francisco, Calif.: Barrett-Koehler, 1997).

[22] Erik H. Erikson, Childhood and Society (New York: Norton, 1963[2]).

[23] Jeff Astley (ed.) *How Faith Grows: Faith Development and Christian Education* (London: National Society/Church House Publishing, 1991).

[24] Patricia O'Connell Killen and John de Beer, *The Art of Theological Reflection* (New York: Crossroad, 2002).

[25] Gibbs and Bolger, *Emerging*, 17.

[26] Murray, *Church*, 19–20.

[27] Alan Jamieson, *A Churchless Faith* (London: SPCK, 2002).

[28] Jo Pimlott, 'Integration and Incarnation: The extent to which creative training activities engender deep learning' (University of Sheffield, 2003, unpublished dissertation).

[29] Trevor Cooling, *Concept Cracking: Exploring Christian Beliefs in School* (Nottingham: Stapleford Project, 1994).

[30] Anne Long, *Approaches to Spiritual Direction* (Cambridge: Grove Books, 1984), 8. Another helpful resource is Ray Simpson, *Soul Friendship: Celtic Insights into Spiritual Mentoring* (London: Hodder & Stoughton, 1999).

[31] See Jon Langford, *Can We Have a Chat? Working Safely With Young People One-to-One* (Cambridge: Grove Books, 2006).

7 – And Finally . . .

[1] Used by permission, Bishop Roger Sainsbury.

[2] Dan Price, *Radical Simplicity* (Philadelphia: Running Press, 2005), 137.